WITHDRAWN

SEP 03 2009

Essential
Barbados

AAA Publishing 1000 AAA Drive, Heathrow, Florida 32746

D0168316

Barbados: Regions and Best places to see

Original text by Lee Karen Stow
Updated by Sue Bryant

American editor: G.K. Sharman

Edited, designed and produced by AA Publishing
© Automobile Association Developments Limited 2008
Maps © Automobile Association Developments Limited 2008

978-1-59508-214-5

Published in the United States by AAA Publishing,
1000 AAA Drive, Heathrow, Florida 32746
Published in the United Kingdom by AA Publishing

Color separation: MRM Graphics Ltd
Printed and bound in Italy by Printer Trento S.r.l.

A03164
Maps in this title produced from:
  map data supplied by Global Mapping, Brackley, UK © 2007
  map data © Borch GmbH
  with additional data from Mountain High Maps® Copyright © 1993 Digital
  Wisdom, Inc

About this book

Symbols are used to denote the following categories:

- ✚ map reference to maps on cover
- ✉ address or location
- ☎ telephone number
- 🕐 opening times
- ✋ admission charge
- 🍴 restaurant or café on premises or nearby
- Ⓜ nearest underground train station
- 🚌 nearest bus/tram route
- 🚃 nearest overground train station
- ⛴ nearest ferry stop
- ✈ nearest airport
- ❓ other practical information
- ℹ tourist information office
- ➤ indicates the page where you will find a fuller description

This book is divided into six sections.

The essence of Barbados pages 6–19
Introduction; Features; Food and drink and Short break

Planning pages 20–33
Before you go; Getting there; Getting around; Being there

Best places to see pages 34–55
The unmissable highlights of any visit to Barbados

Best things to do pages 56–75
Great cafés; stunning views; places to take the children and more

Exploring pages 76–153
The best places to visit in Barbados, organized by area

♦ to ♦♦♦♦ denotes AAA rating

Maps
All map references are to the maps on the covers. For example, Bathsheba has the reference ✚ 4F – indicating the grid square in which it is to be found

Admission prices
Inexpensive (under Bds$15); Moderate (Bds$15–35); Expensive (over Bds$35)

Hotel prices
Prices are per room per night: $ budget (under US$100); $$ moderate (US$100–350); $$$ expensive to luxury (over US$350). Where possible the author has adjusted the rating of all-inclusive hotels to reflect the true quality of the hotel.

Restaurant prices
Price for a three-course meal per person without drinks: $ budget (under Bds$60); $$ moderate (Bds$60–110); $$$ expensive (over Bds$110)

Contents

BEST THINGS TO DO

56 – 75

EXPLORING...

76 – 153

The essence of...

THE ESSENCE OF BARBADOS

Silvery beaches, the warm, translucent, turquoise sea and some of the Caribbean's finest hotels make Barbados one of the world's most desirable holiday destinations. But this is also an island with soul, where gospel singing and the Friday night fish fry are as important as the international polo matches and the annual opera season; a place where cricket is not just a passion, but a national obsession.

Barbados may be less scenically dramatic than some of its volcanic, rainforested neighbors but it is welcoming, safe and rich in colonial history; the perfect place for a relaxing and unforgettable vacation.

features

Barbados enjoys a high repeat visitor factor, but it's not just sun, sea and sand that attracts tourists. Barbadians are known to be among the friendliest people in the Caribbean and visitors who have found the soul of Barbados and forged friendships are those that have been coming back to the island for 20 years or more.

Barbados has gained a reputation as a celebrity hotspot. An eclectic mix of politicians, movie stars, supermodels and musicians all vacation in luxurious private villas and exclusive resorts along the West Coast.

Meanwhile, Barbados and its population of 281,000 carries on as it has done since tourism succeeded the sugar cane industry. Locals and visitors alike enjoy the island's mix of attractions: from natural formations of limestone caves and hidden gullies; beautiful beaches lapped softly by ripples from the Caribbean Sea or swept by the crashing surf of the

Atlantic; to its glittering crop of restaurants and food shacks serving Barbadian (Bajan) food and locally produced rum and beer.

Despite nearly 40 years of independence from Great Britain, a quaint Englishness still exists with cricket on the green, horse racing and afternoon tea. Enriching these traditions are African arts, crafts and songs – the roots unearthed by Barbadians whose ancestors were brought here centuries ago, as slaves to work the sugar plantations.

In 2007 the Cricket World Cup put the island in the spotlight when the final was held in the now state-of-the-art Kensington Oval, and many of the existing attractions were given a face-lift for the big event and the thousands of additional visitors it brought. Although local people faced months of disruption as the island prepared for the visitor invasion, there's a new sense of pride now in Barbados and its ability to host a world-class sporting event.

THE ESSENCE OF BARBADOS

food & drink

Barbadian fare is built on dishes of African origin, spiced up for the Caribbean, with English-inspired, cucumber sandwiches thrown in for good measure.

NATIONAL DISHES

The premier national dish is flying fish, a silvery-blue, sardine-like fish that actually thrashes its tail to enable it to glide above the surface of the sea. Once de-boned, the fish is rolled in breadcrumbs and Bajan seasoning, then deep fried. Other catches of the day are barracuda, dolphin (or dorado, sometimes listed on the menu as *mahi mahi* and a fish, not a dolphin), tuna, kingfish and snapper. Lobster and shrimp harvested in Guyana are grilled and drizzled with oil or smothered in sauces.

Fish is blended into a chowder or battered as fishcakes and served with the island's own hot pepper sauce. Take care with the ubiquitous bottle of

Bajan sauce placed on the table. One dash is enough, three is explosive. For real local food, seek out a cook shop and watch all parts of a chicken, pig or black-bellied sheep go in a pot for simmering. A pudding and souse is actually sausage, sweet potato and boiled pig's head and feet served with cucumber and pepper pickle.

Another national dish is *cou-cou*, made from cornmeal and okra pudding and similar to the African dish *foo foo*. Primarily, the local diet is rich in starch, derived from sweet potatoes, yams and fried plantains (like a banana but must be cooked before eating). Breadfruit was introduced to the island by Captain Bligh of *Mutiny on the Bounty* fame, and pumpkins are made into a delicious soup. Rice mixed with peas is a popular side dish, as is macaroni cheese pie. Look for set-priced Bajan buffets where you help yourself to a dozen typical

dishes. For fast food, Bajans prefer chicken, or a roti filled with meat or fish curry. For dessert, try mango, passion fruit, cherries, papaya, or coconut sweet pie and butter pudding.

ALCOHOLIC DRINKS

A rum shop is a small bar and local haunt where Bajans discuss cricket and politics and play dominoes or the old African game called *warri*. They order a plate of fish and a shot of rum, which comes dark or as clear as pure vodka. The connoisseur usually selects a five-year-old blend. Drink it neat, with crushed ice, with cola, or shaken into a cocktail. Hotels and bars concoct their own mindblowers. Daiquiri is a delicious blend of mango

or banana pulp, rum, lime juice, ice and sugar. Gin and coconut water also goes down well. Banks beer is for

sale everywhere and is best drunk
ice-cold from the bottle.

NON-ALCOHOLIC DRINKS

English afternoon tea served complete
with a tier of cakes, cream scones and
cucumber sandwiches is a west coast
tradition. For sheer refreshment
choose from chilled ginger beer or a
fresh coconut, its top hacked off and a
straw plunged into the milk. *Sorrel* is a
Christmas drink, made from plant
leaves infused in hot water and
spices. Bars sell fruit punches and
real juices, lemonade actually made
from lemons and internationally
known brands of cola and
canned drinks.

TASTY SNACKS

There are plenty of snack items on
Barbados to keep you munching
indulgently between meals. Try
cashew nuts, tamarind balls, jam puffs or nachos with cheese.
You should also taste the freshest bananas sold by the roadside
and a delicious flying fish sandwich known as a *cutter*.

short break

If you only have a short time to visit Barbados, or would like to get a really complete picture of the country, here are the essentials:

● **Spend a day in Bridgetown** (➤ 79) shopping for tax-free jewelry, clothes and handicrafts, then stroll along the riverside boardwalk.

● **Snorkel on the west coast and look for wild turtles,** or go diving to see them glide through the water (➤ 67).

● **Take a picnic to Bathsheba** (➤ 40) on the east coast and watch the waves crash onto the cliffs and beaches.

● **Listen to gospel singing** and enjoy Sunday brunch at The Crane beach hotel (➤ 146), overlooking the dramatic Atlantic coast.

● **Eat fried flying fish and macaroni cheese pie** or rice at the famous Oistins Fish Fry (➤ 148) on Friday and Saturday nights.

- **Take a sunset cruise,** or forget your cares on the lively Jolly Roger party cruise (➤ 96).

- **Visit a rum factory to learn how the national drink is made,** then sample it and purchase a bottle to take home (➤ 133).

- **Ride on an electric tram** through the limestone formations of Harrison's Cave (➤ 48), Barbados's most famous attraction, completely renovated in 2007.

● **Dive to a depth of 147ft (45m) on the Atlantis Submarine** (➤ 144) to see a shipwreck, stingrays, turtles and shoals of colorful tropical fish – without getting wet.

● **Stroll through the terraces of plants** at the Andromeda Botanic Gardens (➤ 36), the extraordinary legacy of one woman.

Planning

Before you go

WHEN TO GO

	JAN	FEB	MAR	APR	MAY	JUN	JUL	AUG	SEP	OCT	NOV	DEC
	27°C	27°C	27°C	27°C	27°C	27°C	31°C	31°C	27°C	27°C	27°C	27°C
	81°F	81°F	81°F	81°F	81°F	81°F	88°F	88°F	81°F	81°F	81°F	81°F

🔴 High season ⚪ Low season

Barbados enjoys a tropical climate with an average daytime high of 75–85°F (24–29°C) and slightly cooler nights. The rainy season is from June to November, with short, sharp showers most afternoons, followed by warm sunshine again. If hurricanes are going to develop, they usually do so between June and October, but Barbados tends to be outside their path as the island is a long way east and separate from the main Caribbean chain of landmasses. The last direct hit was in 1955.

WHAT YOU NEED

● Required
○ Suggested
▲ Not required

Some countries require a passport to remain valid for a minimum period (usually at least six months) beyond the date of entry – contact their consulate or embassy or your travel agency for details.

	UK	Germany	USA	Netherlands	Spain
Passport valid for 6 months beyond date of departure/national ID card	●	●	●	●	●
Visa (regulations can change – check before booking your trip)	▲	▲	▲	▲	▲
Onward or return ticket	●	●	●	●	●
Health inoculations (polio, tetanus, typhoid, hepatitis A)	○	○	○	○	○
Health documentation (► 30, Health)	○	○	○	○	○
Travel insurance	○	○	○	○	○
Driving license (current or international)	●	●	●	●	●
Car insurance certificate (if own car)	○	○	○	○	○
Car registration document (if own car)	▲	▲	▲	▲	▲

WEBSITES

For more information visit: www.barbados.org which is maintained by the Barbados Tourism Authority. Another useful site with general information is: www.visitbarbados.org

TOURIST OFFICES AT HOME

In the UK
Barbados Tourism Authority
263 Tottenham Court Road
London
W1T 7LA
☎ 020 7636 9448

In the USA
Barbados Tourism Authority
800 Second Avenue
2nd Floor
New York
NY 10017
☎ 212 986 6516
Toll Free 1 800 221 9831

HEALTH INSURANCE

If you fall ill, hotels can arrange a doctor to come and see you. If things get serious, the hospital is never far away on this small island. Full medical insurance is highly recommended and should cover you for medical and hospital costs, transportation to a suitable off-island medical facility if required, repatriation and permanent disability. Note that you will need additional coverage for certain sports such as scuba diving.

TIME DIFFERENCES

GMT	Barbados	Germany	USA (NY)	Netherlands	Spain
12 noon	← 8AM	→ 1PM	← 7AM	→ 1PM	→ 1PM

Barbados is four hours behind the UK, five hours in British Summer Time. The island is one hour ahead of East Coast Time. Time does, however, take on different meaning in the Caribbean and visitors should expect to slow their pace accordingly.

NATIONAL HOLIDAYS

January 1 *New Year's Day*
January 22 *Errol Barrow Day*
March or April *Easter*
April 28 *National Heroes Day*

May 1 *Labor Day*
Last Monday in May *Whit Monday*
August 1 *Emancipation Day*
August 6 *Kadooment Day*

November 30 *Independence Day*
December 25 *Christmas Day*
December 26 *Boxing Day*

WHAT'S ON WHEN

December–May Polo season, with fixtures throughout at the island's four fields.

January *Barbados Jazz Festival* One week of live jazz from top artistes like Macy Gray and Anita Baker. At Sunbury Plantation House and Farley Hill.

February *Holetown Festival* A week-long celebration of the first settlement of the island, brought to life with fashion shows, sporting events and parades.

February/March *Gold Cup Festival, Garrison Savannah* The year's most glamorous and prestigious horse race.

March *Holders Season* Two weeks of music, opera and theater at Holders House, St James. A glamorous society event that attracts visitors from all over the world.

April *Fish Festival* A celebration of the fruits of the sea, with dancing, music and a lot of fish at Oistins, the epicenter of the island's fishing industry.

May *Gospelfest*, attracting singers and choirs from all over the Caribbean. *Bridgetown Film Festival.*

July/August *Crop Over* The year's biggest event, traditionally celebrating a successful sugar cane harvest. Five weeks of parades, live bands, calypso music and exhibitions, culminating in the lavish Grand Kadooment carnival parade.

Getting there

BY AIR

Grantley Adams International Airport

9 miles (15km) to city centre

N/A

40 minutes

30 minutes

Barbados is served by, among others, American Airlines, BWIA, Air Jamaica, US Airways, Air Canada, British Airways, Virgin Atlantic, Caribbean Star and LIAT. Visitors arrive at Grantley Adams International Airport in the south. It is the island's only airport and has recently been refurbished. Now, there are shops, exchange facilities and restaurants. British Airways and BWIA offer first- and business-class lounges. Departing passengers pay a tax of US$12.50 or Bds$25.
Airport and flight information ☎ 428 7101; www.gaia.com.bb

BY SEA

Cruise passengers dock at the Deep Water harbor in Bridgetown, at the stylish Cruise Passenger Terminal with duty-free (tax-free) shopping, banking and other facilities.

Getting around

PUBLIC TRANSPORT

Internal flights There are no internal flights within Barbados. Air LIAT, BWIA, American Eagle, Tropicair, Trans Island Air, Air Martinique and Caribe Express operate flights to neighboring islands in the Caribbean.

Helicopters can be chartered for either private transport or "flightseeing" from Bajan Helicopters at the Bridgetown Heliport ☎ 431 0069, www.bajanhelicopters.com

Trains There are no rail services on Barbados.

Buses Buses are an excellent, inexpensive way of getting around. Frequent services run to most parts of the island and all services terminate in Speightstown. A flat fare of Bds$1.50 takes you anywhere. There are two main types of bus: government-owned (blue with a yellow stripe) for which you must have the correct fare, and privately owned mini buses (yellow with a blue stripe) which give change. Destinations are clearly marked on the front or painted on the sides. From Bridgetown, buses run from terminals on Fairchild Street for the south and from Lower Green to the west coast and north. In addition to the main buses there are also the privately owned ZRs, these mini buses, which are white with a maroon stripe, leave from Probyn Street, River Road and Cheapside terminals. For general enquiries ☎ 436 6820.

Boat trips Organized tours of the coastline are available, plus trips to neighboring Caribbean islands.

EXCURSIONS
Numerous companies offer tours of the island; some of them, like Island Safari, in four-wheel drive vehicles, take visitors off-road through the sugar cane fields and along the east coast to beautiful and remote beach spots (➤ 60–61).

If you book a tour, many of the tour companies will pick you up from your hotel. If this is how you plan to see the island, you may not need a car for the entire duration of your stay.

WALKING
The Barbados National Trust organizes regular hikes for three levels of ability, in the morning, afternoon or moonlight. This is a great way to see the island and meet local people. The hikes are free, although donations to the Trust are welcome. For a calendar, visit www.barbados.org/hike1.htm

FARES AND TICKETS
Visitors booking through a tour operator should ask about the Barbados VIP Card, valid from May to November (excluding the Crop Over festival period in July) and offering "Buy one, get one free" deals at most of the main attractions and several restaurants.

Many attractions have two levels of pricing, one for locals and one for visitors. This may seem unfair but it reflects the much lower incomes that local Bajans receive, and the fact that the government encourages locals to make the most of their island.

TAXIS

Cabs may be expensive but they can make sense if there
are a number of you who want to travel around. Identified
by ZR number plates or painted white with a maroon stripe,
the cabs are clean, efficient and many have air conditioning.
There are no meters, but fares are regulated by the
government and published by the tourist office in
Bridgetown. Expect to pay around Bds$30 from the airport
to the south coast, or Bds$75 from the airport to
Speightstown. Taxis can be hired for private tours, too, at
about US$25 per hour. This is often worthwhile as the
drivers are very knowledgeable and are full of gossip and local lore.

DRIVING

- Speed limit on highways: 50mph/80kph
- Speed limit on main roads: 30mph/50kph (inner city 25mph/40kph)
- Speed limit on minor roads: 30mph/50kph (inner city 25mph/40kph)
- Seat belts must be worn at all times and in rear seats where fitted.
- Although there are no specific limits on drinking and driving, you should always drive with due care and attention. You may find that your insurance cover is not valid for accidents due to alcohol.
- Fuel is available in leaded, unleaded, premium and diesel. Bridgetown has one 24-hour fuel station. Others around the island have varying opening and closing times. Most close on Sundays, so you are advised to fill up before you travel at weekends.
- In the event of a breakdown contact your rental agency, which will either send help or replace the vehicle.

CAR RENTAL

Choose anything from a Mini Moke to an air-conditioned sedan. Rent on
arrival at the airport or from your hotel. Vehicles can be hired for an hour,
day, week or longer on production of a current driving license and a major
credit card. You must buy a driving permit for Bds$10, issued from the car
rental companies or the Ministry of Transport ☎ 427 2623. To rent a car,
you must be over 21 and under 75. Bicycles and mopeds are also available
for rent.

Being there

TOURIST OFFICES
The head office of the Barbados
Tourism Authority is on Harbour
Road, Bridgetown and there are
booths at the airport and the cruise
terminal.

MONEY
Barbados's currency is the Barbados dollar (Bds$) which is fixed against
the US dollar (Bds$2=US$1) and divided into 100 cents . Both US and
Barbados dollars are accepted, and major credit cards can be used at
most hotels, restaurants and stores. International banks include Barclays
Bank plc and Canadian Imperial Bank of Commerce. At Grantley Adams
International Airport, the Barbados Bank is open daily from 8am until the
last flight departs.

TIPS/GRATUITIES

Yes ✓ No ✗		
Restaurants (10–15% service usually included)	✗	
Cafés/bars (10% service included)	✗	
Tour guides	✓	US$10
Taxis	✓	10% of the fare
Chambermaids	✓	US$2 per room per day
Cloakroom attendants	✓	US$4
Toilets	✓	change
Porters	✓	US$1 per bag

POSTAL SERVICES
Postal services are good. The main Post Office is in Cheapside,
Bridgetown ☎ 427 5772, open Monday–Friday 8–5. Each parish has its
own smaller post office, usually open 7:30am–12 noon and 1pm–3pm,
and stamps are available from most hotels and book stores as well as the
airport and the cruise terminal. Mail boxes are red.

TELEPHONES

Satellite links and direct dialing are available. All local calls are free except from pay phones where 25 cent coins are needed. Barbados has 95 percent coverage from the Digicel cellular network as well as a couple of other cellular providers. Phones set up for GSM 900, 1800 or 1900 will work on the island. Check roaming costs with your provider at home before traveling.

International dialing codes
From Barbados to:
UK 0 11 44
Germany 0 11 49
USA and Canada 0 11 1
Netherlands 00 11 31

Emergency telephone numbers
Police 211
Fire 311
Ambulance 511 or 911

EMBASSIES AND CONSULATES
UK ☎ 430 7800
Germany ☎ 427 1876
Netherlands ☎ 418 8074
USA ☎ 436 4950

HEALTH ADVICE
Sun advice The Caribbean sun is extremely strong and you must protect your skin. Choose a good-quality, high sun protection factor sunscreen and reapply frequently, especially after swimming and water sports. Avoid the midday sun. Wear good sunglasses and if possible, a wide-brimmed hat. Limit your time in the sun when first going to the beach. If you do suffer sunburn, stay out of the sun until you recover. Beach vendors sell aloe vera, which is very soothing for sunburn. If headache, nausea or dizziness occur, call a doctor.

Drugs Prescriptions and non-prescription drugs and medicines are available from pharmacies.

Safe water Barbados water is very pure, having been filtered by the island's natural coral. It can be enjoyed straight from the tap.

PERSONAL SAFETY

You may be approached and asked to buy marijuana or harder drugs. Politely refuse and walk away. Keep a close eye on belongings and if possible, leave valuables in the hotel safe or room safe. Don't walk the beaches at night and avoid unfamiliar neighborhoods. Don't leave valuables in cars.

ELECTRICITY

The power supply in Barbados is 110 volts 50 cycles. Carry an adapter to make sure your appliances fit the two-prong sockets. Many hotels can also supply adapters.

OPENING HOURS

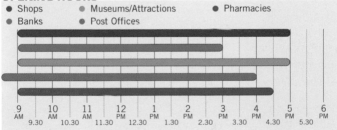

Some stores are also open on Saturday mornings 9–1. Museums are open slightly later in high season. Banks are open 9–5 on Fridays. Pharmacies are also open on Saturdays 8–1. Some do open 24 hours but not all. Check first by phoning a division of the tourist office ☎ 427 2623. There is a clinic on 3rd Avenue Bellivill, on the outskirts of Bridgetown, St Michael which is open until midnight ☎ 228 6120. Other pharmacies include Grants on Fairchild Street, Bridgetown ☎ 436 6120 and in Oistins ☎ 428 9481; and Knights on Lower Broad Street, Bridgetown ☎ 426 5196.

LANGUAGE

Barbados experienced 300 years of British rule and as a result, the official language of the island is English. Everyone speaks and understands English so there is no need to learn the strong and lively West Indian dialect spoken by the local Barbadians (or Bajans as they are also known), and wrongly assumed to be nothing more than broken English. To try to imitate Bajan speak could actually sound false and inappropriate, so it's best to talk normally. Likewise, listening to rapid Bajan speak can be confusing. If you cannot grasp the essence of the conversation, simply ask the speaker to slow down and you'll soon pick up the essential points. Listening to two Bajans in conversation is fascinating, the sound melodic with a distinct laid-back rhythm.

Visitors who insist on learning a few Bajan words however, can buy Learn to Speak Bajan booklets from some souvenir and book stores. The dialect is not difficult to learn. Words such as "three" become "tree," the common "the" is shortened to "de," "them" becomes "dem" and "your" is a spirited "yo" or "yuh." Sometimes the response to a question is a

beautifully rich "doan' know child." Whatever language you speak, though, remember always to remain polite. In Barbados, it is common etiquette to say please, thank you and greet people with a cheerful good morning/ afternoon/evening.

Bajan is a dialect which sounds, although it isn't, like broken English. It is a rich, beautiful language all of its own.

Noticeably common is the replacement of "th" with "de," as in:

wid   – with
den   – then
dey   – they
de   – the
dere   – there
dese   – these

Verbs have no participle endings such as -ed, so a Bajan would say "he fish' instead of "he fished," or "she cook" instead of "she cooked."

Also, the present time is spoken as a real, ongoing thing, for example: "the woman dances to the beat of the steel drum" would be "de woman she dancing to de beat o'de drum." Here are a few wonderful gems to make your ears twitch:

agen	–	again
evaht'ing	–	everything
evaht'ing cook and curry	–	everything's all taken care of
dat ol talk	–	idle gossip
a pot o'Bajan soup	–	a dish of stew
boil up	–	bring to the boil
cook up	–	all ingredients are cooked together
limin	–	hanging around
piece o'pumpkin and piece o'pigtail	–	ingredients for the pot
if greedy wait, hot will cool	–	wait until the dish cools and you can eat
the sea en' got no back door	–	if you get into a mess, you might not get out of it
big bout yah	–	you got fame/money/looks/talent

Best places to see

1 Andromeda Botanic Gardens

A profusion of both indigenous and tropical plants and flowers pays tribute to the mythical Greek princess Andromeda in this garden by the ocean.

Bathsheba (➤ 40), on the rugged eastern coastline, makes a dramatic setting for this garden established in 1954 by the late amateur horticulturist Mrs Iris Bannochie. Mrs Bannochie devoted herself to the garden, creating trails of blossoms and tropical foliage on the cliffs above the Atlantic, and collected many rare species of plant on her trips around the world. She named her creation after Andromeda (daughter of King Cepheus of Ethiopia) who, according to legend, was chained at the water's edge as a sacrifice to the sea monster before being rescued by Perseus.

Cascading streams and waterfalls have been added, and the gardens are building up a collection of medicinal plants with information on their traditional uses. Andromeda is astonishingly beautiful, awash with frangipani (*Plumeria rubra*), bougainvillaea (*Bougainvillaea spectabilis*), traveler's trees (*Ravenala madagascariensis*) and orchids (*Orchidaceae*). Through strategically scattered palms you

glimpse the azure blue of the ocean from viewpoints on the pathways. The fishing village in the distance is Tent Bay. As you admire Andromeda, Barbados monkeys swing in the trees above, and there are mongooses and lizards.

In 1988, before her death, Iris Bannochie donated her gardens to the Barbados National Trust. The Trust now offers tours led by knowledgeable volunteer horticulturists on Wednesdays at 10:30am. If you prefer to go it alone, there's a choice of two self-guided trails, one covering hilly areas and taking up to an hour, and the other a half-hour, easier stroll.

🕇 4F ⊠ Bathsheba, St Joseph ☎ 433 9261 or 433 9384 ⓒ Daily 9–5 (except public holidays) 🖐 Moderate, children half price 🍴 Light meals, snacks and afternoon tea served at the Hibiscus Café ($$). The cook will also prepare a picnic lunch for you to eat in the gardens 🚌 From Bridgetown, Speightstown ❓ Further information from the Barbados National Trust (☎ 426 2421, http://trust.funbarbados.com)

2 Barbados Wildlife Reserve

www.barbadodmonkey.com

This natural mahogany forest, home to exotic animals, birds and reptiles, also features buildings made of coral stone and relics of the sugar industry.

While sipping a cold drink at the mahogany bar here, don't be surprised to see a red-footed Barbados tortoise stroll by. Except for caged parrots and a python, the animals here mostly roam freely over the 4 acres (1.5ha) of forest. The reserve is built from coral stone gathered from surrounding canefields and its paths are made of bricks (still carrying the manufacturer's stamp) from 17th- and 18th-century sugar factories.

Children love it here, but they must be supervised as some of the animals, including the monkeys, can bite. Among the mix are cattle egrets, spectacled caimans, guinea fowl, deer, pelicans, congas, flamingos, cockatoos, toucans and peacocks. In a straw-carpeted pen, iguanas of the West Indies, the largest vertebrates native to the Caribbean islands, sprawl on logs. They bake in the sun, oblivious to the rabbits hopping

around them and the juvenile tortoises crawling by. Many creatures arrived here as gifts to the reserve. The agoutis and the armadillos are from the forestry departments in St Lucia and St Vincent, while the pelicans hail from Florida.

To see the Barbados green (or vervet) monkeys, be here between 2 and 3pm, when the colony returns from the forests of nearby Grenade Hall (➤ 108). Originally introduced from West Africa, the monkeys number around 5,000–7,000 on the island and just one animal can provide up to 2.5 million doses of polio vaccine. The reserve's Primate Research Center, focusing on the use and conservation of the monkey, is responsible for up to 70 percent of the world's production of the vaccine.

✚ 2E ✉ Farley Hill, St Peter ☎ 422 8826 🕐 Daily 10–5 (last admission 3:45) ✋ Moderate, children half price. Includes admission to Grenade Hall Forest and Signal Station 🍴 Café ($) 🚌 Continuous bus service from Bridgetown, Holetown, Speightstown and Bathsheba ❓ Several sightseeing operators visit the reserve

3 Bathsheba

This tiny beauty spot on the east coast has a great appeal for those wanting to see the rugged, natural face of Barbados.

There are no luxury hotels at Bathsheba and you won't find anyone to park your car. Even in peak season, this fishing village is devoid of crowds. Its coves and bays are washed by excellent surf and surfing champions ride the waves from September to December at the frothy Soup Bowl at the center of the beach. Two rows of giant, grass-covered boulders seem to guard the bay from the threat of the approaching tide. In fact, apart from the bathing pools that fill up and can be enjoyed at low tide, it's far too dangerous to swim here.

What you can do, though, is stroll by the church and the pastel-painted houses or wander along the deserted beaches backed by chalky cliffs and wild hills. There are no formal attractions here, just the peace and scenery. Nearby are the green hills of Cattlewash, so-called because the cattle wander down to the ocean to take a bath.

In Victorian times, Bathsheba was a magnet for vacationing

Barbadians who would
come to take the air.
A railroad ran from
Bridgetown to
Bathsheba from 1883
until it closed in 1937.
Its life was precarious,
suffering from landslides, underfunding and
mismanagement. Coastal erosion was so bad the
crew often had to get out to repair the track.

✚ 4F 🍴 New Edgewater Hotel ($) – for the Sunday Bajan
buffet, 12–3, book in advance (➤ 121) 🚌 Continuous bus
service from Bridgetown, Holetown and Speightstown

4 Chalky Mount Village

www.highland-pottery.com

You can watch pottery being made and fired traditionally and enjoy fabulous views of the Scotland District in the chalk hills of St Andrew.

The skilled potter Winston Junior Paul and his wife, Prim, run Highland Pottery, a uniquely placed workshop high in Chalky Mount Village. It stands on a geological formation said to resemble a sleeping man with his hands folded over his stomach. Locals refer to it as "Napoleon." At one time over 20 pottery businesses thrived here, the studios and workshops humming in wood houses high on the hills. Today, only a couple struggle to make a living, battling against cheap imports. Beneath them is the brown-red clay dug to create the artists' pieces. Winston's workshop is like a tree house, open on all sides to let in the

refreshing breezes. It has a 360-degree view of the undulating eastern landscape, known as the Scotland District, that rambles down to the Atlantic.

Winston tells you how the clay is first mixed with water then sieved to take out the tree roots. The mixture is then laid out on drying trays in the sun for about three weeks until the water has evaporated. Next it is brought indoors where the rushing wind dries out the last of the water. He invites you to watch him knead the clay on the wedging table, squeezing out the bubbles before slapping it down on the potter's wheel. Before the advent of electricity, pots were thrown on a kick wheel, which is made of cement and shaped like a millstone. The wheel is kicked to rotate the clay and Winston is so skilled at it that he appears to be running while shaping a flower vase before your eyes. He then fires the pots in the kiln, after which they are painted and glazed and displayed on shelves.

🚹 3F ✉ Chalky Mount Potteries, Chalky Mount, Scotland District ☎ 431 0747, 🕐 Daily 9–5 ✋ Free 🍴 Restaurants/cafés ($–$$) at Bathsheba 🚌 From Bridgetown

5 Flower Forest and Orchid World

This colorful duo, featuring tropical and native trees and spectacular orchids, lies on a popular scenic route in the parishes of St Joseph and St John.

Flower Forest

Set 846ft (258m) above sea level on a former sugar plantation, the 50-acre (20ha) forest has a visitor center furnished with old copper sugar-boiling vats and decorated with a mural depicting the plantation's history. From here a nature trail leads through a tropical corridor of neatly labeled plants and trees. Look for the native bearded fig tree *(Ficus citrifolia)*, bamboos and breadfruit *(Artocarpus altilis)*, plus the Queen of Flowers tree, which was planted by Princess Alexandra in 1992. Some rest spots overlook manicured lawns, the most splendid being Liv's Lookout, with views of the rugged Scotland District and the island's highest point, Mount Hillaby, at 1,115ft (340m).

Orchid World

Opened by Prime Minister Owen Arthur in 1998, Orchid World lies in the high rainfall area of the island, which averages 79in (203cm) annually. Rainwater is collected in a 29,920-gal (136,000 liter) tank and, as much as possible, recycled. This makes for a healthy environment for a plethora of orchid species that is continually being added to. Orchids spring up everywhere, and *vandas*, *schomburgkia* and *oncidium* grow by the paths. *Epiphytes*, or air plants, dangle from wire frames in the specially controlled environment of the orchid houses. Coral, limestone rockeries, caves and a babbling stream add to the tranquillity of the garden, which has a far-reaching view across the silvery sheen of the sugar cane fields.

Flower Forest
✚ 3F ✉ Richmond, St Joseph ☎ 433 8152 ⏱ Daily 9–5 (last tour 4pm) ✋ Moderate 🍴 On site café ($) 🚌 From Bridgetown take the Chalky Mount or Sugar Hill bus and ask the driver to drop you off near the forest

Orchid World
✚ 3H ✉ Between Gun Hill and St John's Church, Highway 3b ☎ 433 0306 ⏱ Daily 9–5 (last admission 4:30) ✋ Moderate 🍴 Café ($) 🚌 From Bridgetown take the Sargeant Street bus

6 Garrison Historic Area

Once the defense nucleus of Barbados, the Garrison consists of a circle of mid-17th century military buildings and an exceptional cannon collection.

When Oliver Cromwell took control of England after the Civil War of 1648, he set his sights on Barbados. But Lord Willoughby, the governor of Barbados, decided to strengthen the island's defense. Needham's Fort, later renamed Charles Fort, today

stands as the oldest building, dating back to 1650. It was strengthened by the addition of another fort, St Ann's, now the headquarters of the Barbados Defense Force.

When France declared war on Britain in 1778, an influx of British troops arrived at the Garrison. The bewildered Barbados government, which had trouble finding enough accommodations for them, were forced to build temporary barracks. The majority of troops left when the war ended. A permanent garrison building was built to accommodate the soldiers who stayed and to prevent future attacks on the British islands. Over the years the Garrison has seen many alterations but the distinctive redbrick clock

tower of the Main Guard has changed little. The 30 or so 17th- to 18th-century cannons, from perhaps the world's largest collection, are housed within the Barbados Defense Force Compound at St Ann's Fort.

Since the withdrawal of the British troops from Barbados in 1905–1906, some buildings have been refurbished. The latest to receive attention is Bush Hill House where the United States' first president, George Washington, stayed in 1751. The house is now known as George Washington House and is open to the public (➤ 143). St Ann's Fort and the Main Guard are also being restored.

Horse racing takes place on the Garrison Savannah, the former parade ground. By day cricket teams practice their batting and fielding, while locals jog around the track. It was here, on November 20, 1966, that the British Union Flag was lowered and Barbados's blue and gold flag – bearing a trident – raised to mark Independence Day.

➕ 2K ✉ St Michael 🏛 Free 🍴 Brown Sugar ($$) (➤ 147) 🚌 From Bridgetown and the south coast ❓ 1.5-hour tours of the Garrison area. Own transport needed ☎ 427 1436

7

Harrison's Cave

www.harrisonscave.com

A ride on an electric tram takes you through the subterranean stream passages of a natural limestone wonder – the island's most famous site.

A labyrinth of creamy white stalagmites and stalactites dripping with rainwater, Harrison's Cave is a world away from the tropical jungle above it. Deep below the island's geographical center, you don a hard hat and hop aboard a trolley car for a 1-mile (1.5-km) long guided tour. Following a smooth underground passageway, you halt to photograph the "cathedral" chamber, a waterfall pouring into an 8-ft (2.5-m) deep pool. Nearby is a group of conical shapes known as "people's village." Alongside runs the original subterranean stream. Above hangs the "chandelier," continuously dripping with calcite-laden water. The stalactites and stalagmites have been growing over thousands of years and in some places have joined together to form pillars.

Although named after Thomas Harris who owned most of the land in the area during the early 1700s, the caves were actually discovered in 1796 by Dr George Pinckard, an English doctor who lived on the island. Several expeditions were attempted during the 18th and 19th centuries but with little success and it was not until the 1970s that the true extend of this natural wonder was revealed by a Danish speleologist and Barbadian cavers. Government-backed explorations and excavations followed and an underground stream was diverted as work on creating an attraction began.

The first tourists arrived in 1981 and the cave has since welcomed Queen Elizabeth II and musicians Paul McCartney and Elton John. The full story of the caves and how they were discovered is explained in an audiovisual show in a special theater, shown before the tour gets underway.

The cave is one of the island's "must see" sights. The surrounding facilities were completely refurbished for the 2007 Cricket World Cup and there's a new Interpretation Center, restaurant and souvenir shop.

✚ 3G ✉ Welchman Hall, St Thomas
☎ 438 6640 🕐 Tours daily at half-hourly intervals. First tour 9:00, last tour 4
✋ Moderate 🍴 Snack bar ($–$$) on site
🚌 Bus from Bridgetown marked Shorey Village

8 National Heroes Square, Bridgetown

Originally planned to represent London's Trafalgar Square in miniature, the capital's focal point is becoming increasingly Barbadian.

Before April 28, 1999, this main square was known as Trafalgar Square, a throwback to the days when Barbados was known as Little England. The square was renamed by the prime minister, Owen Arthur, in a ceremony that took place to mark the occasion of the second National Heroes Day. It is a holiday

that remembers notable figures in the island's history. Taxi drivers and locals, however, still call it Trafalgar Square.

During the ceremony, 10 people were honored, including Errol Walton Barrow, the first prime minister elected after independence in 1966; Bussa, the slave leader of the 1816 rebellion; cricket star Sir Garfield Sobers; and Samuel Jackman Prescod. Prescod, the son of a slave mother, rose in 1843 to become the country's first non-white member of Parliament in more than 200 years. He fought for the rights of all classes and colors.

A bronze statue of Lord Nelson was erected in the square in 1813. Nelson sailed to the island in 1805 with a large fleet, which included the *Victory*, months before he perished at the Battle of Trafalgar. For decades there has been talk of moving Nelson (he's considered as a defender of the slave trade) elsewhere and erecting a Barbadian figure, possibly that of Barrow, instead.

Opposite the admiral towers the obelisk honoring the Barbadians killed in World Wars I and II. In the center, the Dolphin Fountain commemorates the first running water piped to the town. Surrounding the square are the neo-Gothic buildings of the seat of Parliament, including the Treasury and House of Assembly (➤ 82). This is an ideal starting point for your own walking tour of the capital.

✚ *Bridgetown 5d* ✉ Junction of Broad Street and St Michael's Row, Bridgetown, St Michael ✋ Free
🍴 Numerous cafés and restaurants ($–$$) on Broad Street and along the Careenage 🚌 All buses run to Bridgetown

9 Speightstown

Brightly colored fishing boats, wooden houses and a quaint church make up this typical West Indian settlement, Barbados's second biggest town.

Speightstown (pronounced "Spitestown") might appear sleepy, but the calm is broken when the fishing boats come in and locals arrive to shop. It bears a history as a thriving port for sugar and the old commercial part is gradually being restored by the Barbados National Trust. The beautiful Arlington House, one of the National Trust's properties, is due to open to the public as an interpretive center in 2008 with the theme "Trading Memories". There's also a smart new marina, Port St Charles, now home to several gleaming yachts.

The town offers modern shopping in the Mall, bakeries serving Bajan bread, and market stalls of fruit and vegetables. There's also the chance to while away the hours in a rum shop with the Bajans on a Saturday afternoon, listening to cricket on the radio.

Founded by William Speight, Speightstown was the principal export destination for the island's sugar. Because of the town's importance, military forts were built around it for protection but today little remains of this defensive ring.

St Peter's Parish Church, one of the earliest churches on the island, dates from around 1630. Inside, the wooden gallery above was once occupied by the "poor whites," the name given to descendants of English, Irish and Scots who were imported as indentured labor to work on the sugar cane plantations.

A "Round de Town" stroll and the longer, more challenging award winning Arbib Nature and Heritage Trail (➤ 118) organized by the Barbados National Trust both begin by the painted blue benches at the harborside, just past the Fisherman's pub.

✚ 1E ✉ Speightstown, St Peter 🚌 Buses from all over the island ❓ A 2-hour "Round de Town" stroll runs on Wed, Thu and Sat (or by alternative arrangement) from 9am or 2:30pm, depending on numbers (☎ 426 2421 💧 Moderate)

10 Sunbury Plantation House

Bordered by gardens, this 340-year-old plantation house is crammed to the ceiling with relics from the days of the great white sugar planters.

For the best insight into how the wealthy white planters lorded it up while their slaves and laborers sweated, step inside Sunbury Plantation House. You're immediately surrounded by trappings of the rich, an outstanding collection of Victorian and Edwardian pottery, silverware and china. Anywhere else such a trove would be roped off or protected behind glass show cabinets. At Sunbury, where all the rooms are accessible, you walk among the Barbados mahogany tables and antiques as though you're waiting for the owner to return.

Originally thought to be called Chapmans after one of the first planter families, Sunbury is now owned by Mr and Mrs Keith Melville. They opened the house to the public in 1983. Highlights include the sunroom, furnished with a white rattan suite, where the ladies would mingle. Men conducted business in the office, the only room to contain the house's original curios, including a 1905 calculator. Portraits of wealthy landowners hang alongside drawings of scenes from the West Indies during the days of slavery. Upstairs, the airy bedrooms are a treat. Check out the 1920s swimming costume, the marble hip bath and the lady's silver brush set on the dressing table.

✚ 4J ✉ St Philip ☎ 423 6270 🕐 Daily 9:30–4:30
✋ Moderate 🍴 Courtyard restaurant and bar ($–$$)
🚌 From Oistins to College Savannah or Bayfield
❓ A planter's candlelit dinner at Sunbury includes a five-course meal, cocktails, all drinks and a tour of the house. Reservations required. Minimum number of 10.

Best things to do

Good places to have lunch

Brown Sugar ($$–$$$)

Beautiful setting on a fern-filled patio with cool splashing water. Creole fish chowder, pepper chicken and coconut beer shrimp are specialties (➤ 147).

🖂 St Michael ☎ 426 7684; www.brownsugarbarbados.com

💎 Bubba's Sports Bar and Restaurant ($)

Local dishes, seafood and international kids' meals as well as fajitas, pasta, salads and burgers (➤ 147).

🖂 Rodeley, Christ Church ☎ 435 6217; www.bubbassportsbar.net

💎💎💎 Cobblers Cove ($$$)

The Terrace restaurant within this Relais et Chateaux hotel is set right on the waterfront and ideal for a special occasion. Reservations required (➤ 120).

🖂 Cobbler's Cove, St Peter ☎ 422 2291; www.cobblerscove.com

Hibiscus Café ($–$$)

Light meals, snacks or a picnic lunch to eat in the gardens (➤ 36–37).

🖂 Andromeda Botanic Gardens ☎ 433 9261 or 433 9384

Mannie's Suga Suga Beach Bar ($$–$$$)

Light lunches overlooking the beach. Salads, sandwiches, grills and "rum shop specialties" right on the beach in Mullins Bay (➤ 123).

🖂 Mullins Bay, St Peter ☎ 419 4511

New Edgewater Hotel ($$)

Cliffside restaurant with Bajan buffet and views over the ocean from the mahogany deck (➤ 41, 121).

🖂 Bathsheba, St Joseph ☎ 433 9900

Patisserie Flindt ($)

Pretty café, run by Savoy-trained chef Carsten Flindt; perfect for an afternoon treat of fabulous cake or ice cream (➤ 124).

✉ Holetown, St James ☎ 432 2626; www.flindtbarbados.com

Ship Inn ($)

Tasty Bajan buffet or huge à la carte menu. Informal and lively, especially in the evenings (➤ 148–149).

✉ St Lawrence Gap, Christ Church ☎ 420 7447; www.shipinnbarbados.com

Best beaches

Barbados has around 69 miles (112km) of coastline and public beaches. The west is calm enough for swimming, snorkeling and water skiing; the south is for windsurfing; and the east is the domain of experienced surfers and body boarders only, and for spectacular photography.

WEST COAST

Fitts Village offers good snorkeling and is within reach of the Malibu Beach Club, which has its own beach, offering water sports and beach volleyball. A visitor center shows you how Malibu rum is made.

   Paynes Bay has palm trees growing out of the sand and hawkers selling sarongs, shirts, Reggae hats, sunglasses, coconuts and sun loungers.

Mullins Bay is a busy favorite where you can do anything, from snorkeling to whizzing around on a jet ski. Sit in a deck chair and have your hair beaded, sunbathe, or perch on a stool at the bamboo bar and sip a cocktail. Gibbes Bay to the south is quieter.

SOUTH COAST
Accra Beach is usually packed with well-toned people sunbathing, strutting around or body surfing. It's great for posing and people-watching.

Sandy Beach (also called Rockley Beach) is ideal for families with children as it is protected by a reef that creates a shallow lagoon calm enough for swimming and snorkeling. You can also get to grips with windsurfing before progressing to Silver Sands.

Breezy **Silver Sands** (► 141) at the southern tip of the island is home to windsurfing experts, though intermediate windsurfers can take lessons. It is a refreshing place with much water sport activity.

EAST COAST
Crane Bay is beloved for its high cliffs plunging down to pink-tinged sands and a white-tipped ocean, apparently perfect for surfing.

At **Bottom Bay,** admire the views then head down the cliff steps and weave through the palms that decorate the white sands. This is one of the most beautiful spots on the island.

Bathsheba (► 40) is pounded by the Atlantic Ocean and scattered with strange boulders. Breathtaking it is, though the current makes it too dangerous for swimming.

Places to take the children

Atlantis Submarine

A real submarine taking day and night dives to the bottom of the
ocean, with views of coral gardens, wrecks and tropical fish
(► 144). If you are lucky you might see a turtle swimming by.
Children are awarded a certificate after the dive.

✉ Shallow Draught, Bridgetown ☎ 436 8929; www.atlantisadventures.com

Barbados Wildlife Reserve

Watch tortoises roam freely around the reserve and rabbits hop
around the iguanas in the pen. Barbados green monkeys are often
seen swinging through the trees around 2–3pm when food is laid
out for them (► 38).

✉ Farley Hill, St Peter ☎ 422 8826 🕐 Daily 10–5 (3:45 last admission)

Harbour Master Cruise

Lunchtime cruise along the coast on a huge, four-deck vessel with
onboard craft demonstrations, Bajan food and best of all, a 70-foot
(21m) water slide.

☎ 430 0900, www.tallshipscruises.com

Harrison's Cave

Stalactites, stalagmites and an electric tram ride underground that
children will love. Reopening in 2008 after a huge refurbishment,
this is one of the islands best attractions (► 48).

✉ Welchman Hall, St Thomas ☎ 438 6640; www.harrisonscave.com

Ocean Park

This new aquarium attraction, geared toward families, takes an
educational slant. See fish and marine life from the Caribbean, a
living reef, ray pool and touch pool and feeding demonstrations
(► 135).

✉ Balls, Christ Church ☎ 420 7405 🕐 Summer Tue–Sun 10–6; winter
daily 10–5

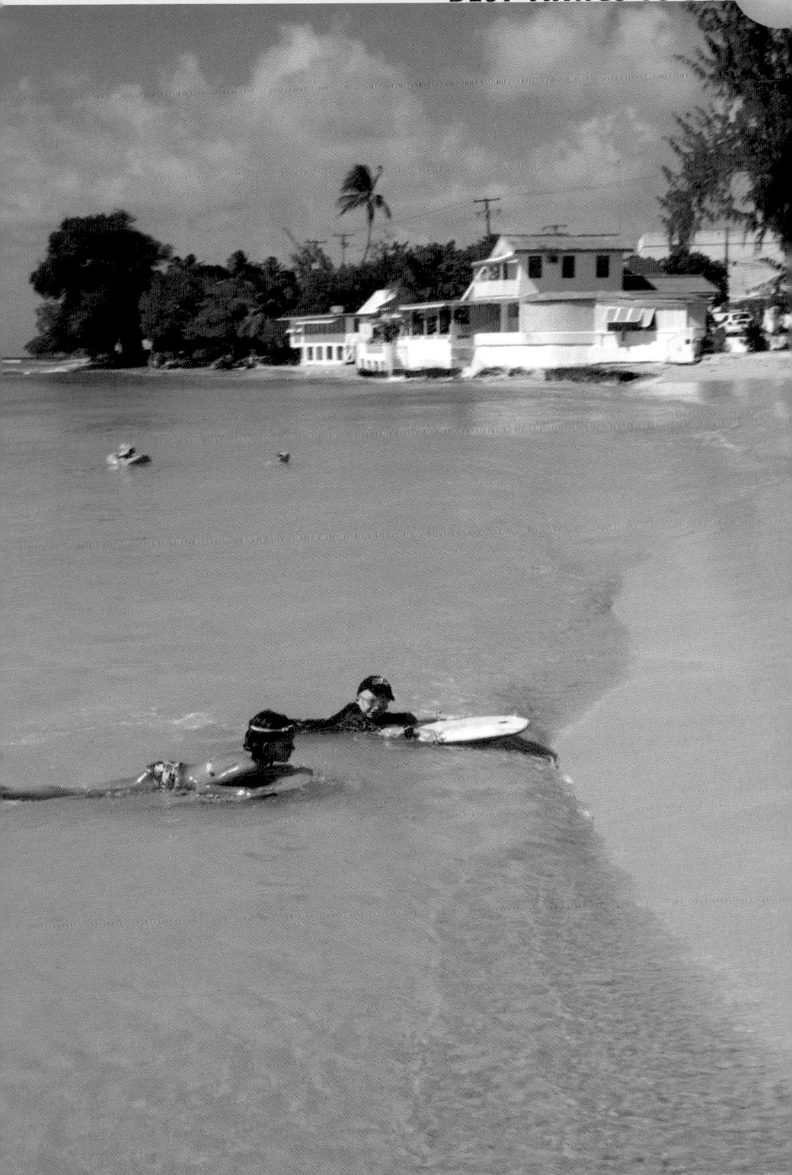

a walk to Mullins Bay

An easy-going stroll along the beach punctuated by swimming and sunning, and ending with a fantastic sunset. The walk is mainly on the beach but there are some stretches of road involved.

From Speightstown (➤ 52), follow the lane leading to the beach and turn left into the curve of a cove, overlooked by the Cobbler's Cove Hotel (➤ 74).

Here early evening strollers may have witnessed the mass exodus of turtle hatchlings, heading from their nests to the ocean. If you come across baby turtles, don't handle them

as they will become disoriented and may never find the water. Just before Cobbler's Cove is a river outlet where cheerful vendors sell Hawaiian-style shirts and sarongs.

Wander along the beach littered with fragments of bone-white coral, passing sunbathers on loungers outside the King's Beach Hotel.

Notice the occasional coconut palms bending almost horizontally to the water. On Barbados everything from this tree is used. The fruit makes a coconut drink, the flesh is scraped and used in baking scones (biscuits), the husk for souvenirs, the trunk for building houses and the palm fronds for weaving baskets.

Pass wooden beach shacks where women sit outside and scrape the scales off fish. You may see the square fishing baskets that are left on the seabed for days until the fish swim in and become trapped. Often there is a fisherman at the shoreline casting out his fishing net.

Rounding the corner you'll see the full stretch of Mullins Bay, and a small market selling beachwear. This is a good place to sit at the beach bar and drink a piña colada before retracing your steps back along the beach. Or you could return along the coastal road, or take the bus.

Distance 0.62 miles (1km)
Time Half to a full day with swimming and stops
Start Point Speightstown beach ✚ 1E
End Point Mullins Bay ✚ 1F
Lunch Mannie's Suga Suga Beach Bar ($$–$$$) (➤ 58) ✉ Mullins Bay ☎ 419 4511

Top places for diving

Barbados is a coral limestone island and as such, has some wonderful underwater scenery, with both fringe and barrier coral reefs in dazzling colors, teeming with life including schools of silvery jacks, big eels, sea horses, frog fish and barracuda. Divers will also encounter graceful rays and gentle Hawksbill turtles, shadowy figures gliding beneath the dive boats in search of tidbits.

The two main dive areas are the calm, Caribbean west and south coasts; the Atlantic Ocean to the east is too rough and the coral less impressive. There are numerous dive schools located around Carlisle Bay, reputedly the location of 200 wrecks, many of them at depths shallow enough to be accessible to novice and inexperienced divers. Most of the wrecks can be reached from the shore, two of the most popular being the *Stavronikita* and the *Pamir*, and a large part of the bay has been designated a Marine Park. Some of the deeper wrecks, at around 160ft (50m) and better suited to experienced divers, are of old sailing ships, with fascinating debris like ancient wine bottles scattered on the seabed.

Dive schools in Barbados cater for both PADI and BSAC-qualified divers and will train beginners to gain PADI certification (which is easier than the stringent and superior BSAC courses). There's really no better place to learn, with beautifully clear, warm water, amazing colors and easy conditions a short distance from the shore. At very least, be sure to take out a mask and snorkel and admire some of the vibrantly colored tropical fish from above.

Stunning views

- Bathsheba (➤ 40)

- Cherry Tree Hill (➤ 111)

- Cove Bay

- Gun Hill (➤ 132)

- Hackleton's Cliff

- Mullins Bay (➤ 61, 64–65)

- North Point (➤ 111)

- Ragged Point (➤ 136)

- Royal Westmoreland Golf Course

- Silver Sands (➤ 61, 141)

a drive along the ABC Highway

A drive along the modern Adams Barrow Cummins Highway (ABC) is a journey through Barbados's history. Many commuters head in and out of Bridgetown daily, so avoid morning and evening traffic. At lunchtime the traffic situation is better, and Sundays are ideal. The highway links the Grantley Adams International Airport with the west coast road, the Ronald Mapp Highway, up to Speightstown. It is named after three of the island's statesmen: Tom Adams (prime minister from 1976 to 1985); Errol Barrow (prime minister from 1966 to 1976 and 1986 to 1987); and Gordon Cummins (premier from 1958 to 1961).

Start at the roundabout near the University of the West Indies and take the ABC marked route, heading east.

You'll see traditional scenery of cane fields and chattel houses contrasting with the sleek buildings of telecommunications companies, car showrooms, banks and the island's television station. At the top of the St Barnabas Highway is the Freed Slave, also known as Bussa or the Emancipation Statue. A heroic figure in the island's history, Bussa was blamed for leading the slave rebellion of 1816 in which many were killed, executed or deported. So long as you park safely and take care crossing the roundabout, you can reach the steps up to the statue base to take a photo.

Back at the roundabout, you can take a detour west along Two Mile Hill toward Government House, once the home of John Pilgrim, a Quaker. The governor of Barbados lives there now. Get back on the ABC Highway and head south along St Barnabas Highway to the Garfield Sobers Roundabout. At the next roundabout (Errol Barrow) go straight on to St Lawrence Gap (➤ 140), a hive of souvenir shops, bars and cafés.

Park and explore the Gap or go birdwatching in the Graeme Hall Bird Sanctuary (➤ 130).

Distance 5 miles (8km)
Time 2 hours
Start Point Roundabout near University of the West Indies ✚ 1J
End Point St Lawrence Gap ✚ 2K
Lunch Excellent choice in St Lawrence Gap ($–$$$) (➤ 147–149)

Top activities

● Watch a game of cricket, the national passion of Barbados.

● Bet on the horses at the historic Garrison Savannah (➤ 47).

● Snorkel with the turtles – but don't feed them.

● Dive the coral reefs and wrecks (➤ 67).

● Go on a four-wheel drive adventure safari, the perfect way to get an insider's view of Barbados.

● Take a Sunday stroll with the Barbados National Trust and learn about local mythology and history (➤ 27) or take one of their guided walks in Andromeda Botanic Gardens every Wednesday (➤ 37).

● Hop aboard a yacht and feel like a millionaire for a day.

● Try your swing at one of the golf courses, which range from basic pay-and-play to world-class championship layouts (➤ 126, 153).

● Go horseback riding.

● Learn to body board in the gentle rollers off the south coast.

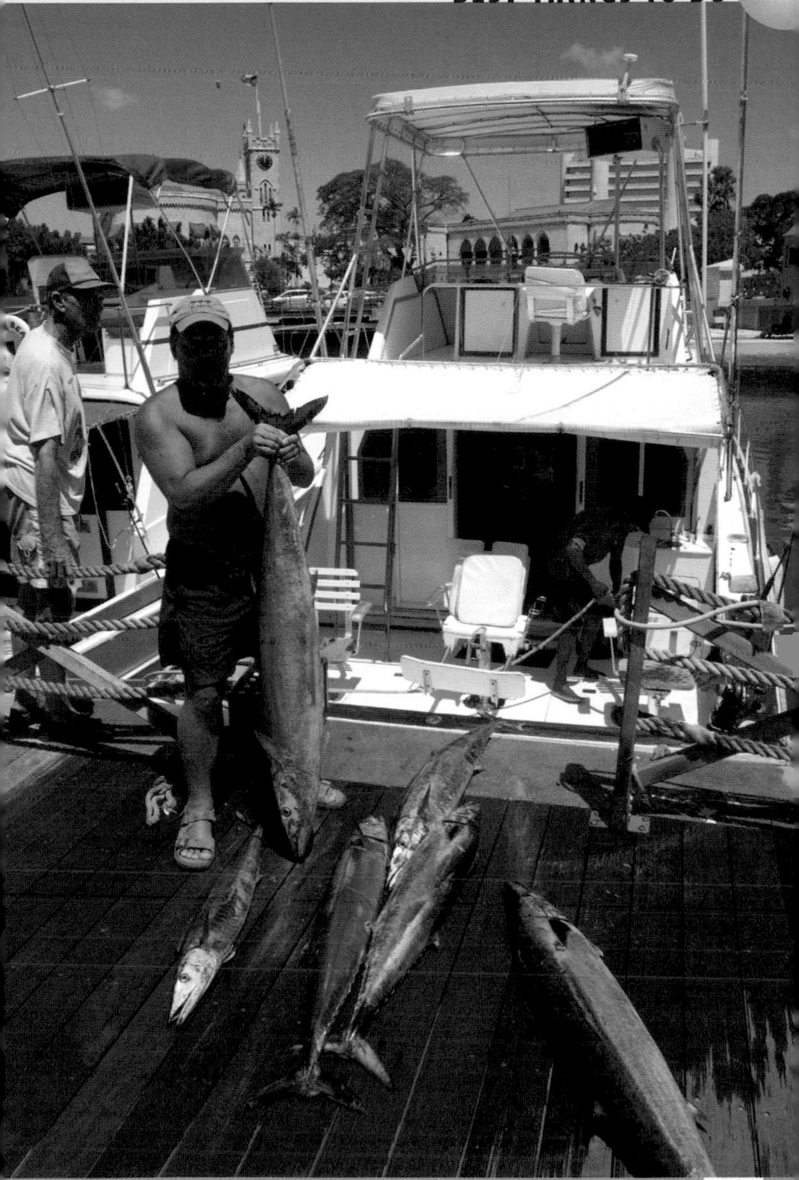

Best places to stay

🔱🔱🔱Almond Beach Village ($$–$$$)
Large all-inclusive property divided into several areas, for couples, families, luxury and so on. Numerous pools and beautiful beach. Superb childcare and many dining options (➤ 120).

🔱🔱🔱Cobblers Cove ($$$)
Country house-style hotel on the west coast with beautiful colonial décor, wonderful food and an English feel. The Terrace restaurant is one of the most romantic on the island (➤ 58, 120).

🔱🔱🔱Coral Reef Club ($$)
Stay in coral stone cottages surrounding a pretty, plantation-style house. The hotel has been owned by the same family for five decades and the service, as a result, is impeccable (➤ 120).

♦♦Crystal Cove Hotel ($$)

All-inclusive hotel for families, with a children's club and a gently sloping beach. The three-tiered lagoon pool is spectacular (➤ 120).

♦♦♦♦The Fairmont Royal Pavilion Hotel ($$$)

Luxury resort hotel set in beautiful, lush gardens on the west coast (➤ 121).

♦♦♦The House at Tamarind Cove ($$$)

Adults-only retreat with 34 simply decorated suites, wonderful service and the wonderful Daphne's restaurant on site (➤ 121).

♦♦♦Lone Star Restaurant and Hotel ($$$)

Just four simple but luxurious suites and the new Beach House,

which attracts an A-list clientele, belonging to the legendary Lone Star bar and restaurant (➤ 123).

♦♦♦The Sandpiper ($$)

Boutique hotel in Holetown, set in tropical gardens and fronting onto a sandy beach. Sister hotel of the Coral Reef Club, with which it shares facilities (➤ 121).

♦♦♦♦Sandy Lane ($$$)

The *grande dame* of Barbados hotels. Lavish in every way, with spectacular spa, impressive children's club, enormous lagoon pool and exclusive dining (➤ 121).

Treasure Beach ($$)

Intimate, popular hotel with 35 suites in traditional Caribbean architectural style, set in a horseshoe shape around the pretty pool. The deluxe suites have private plunge pools (➤ 122).

Exploring

Settled by Arawak Indians, who harvested the rich fishing grounds, the north is the least developed part of the island today. Millions of blades of sugar cane, silvery in the sunlight, bend toward the white surf. Similarly unspoiled is the east coast, with the hilly Scotland District plunging down to sand and palm beaches.

The south and west are the tourist hubs, each very different in character – and price. Bridgetown is the busiest place on the island; particularly so when the big cruise ships arrive in port, mainly in the winter months. In contrast, rising up to the highlands in the center of the island are patches of tropical forest above limestone caves.

It's possible to drive around the island in one day, but you'd be wiser exploring sections at a time and taking a long lunch, out of the midday heat. Alternatively, round up some friends for a swim: a beach is never far away.

Bridgetown

Bridgetown

The town was originally known as Indian River Bridge, after the discovery of an Amerindian bridge that spanned the Constitution River here. Founded by British settlers in 1628, it grew up to become the island's administrative and commercial capital and principal port. Before independence in 1966 Bridgetown bowed under British sovereignty, which is why you'll detect traces of English character in its colonial architecture. Bridgetown, with the sumptuously furnished houses of the sugar planters and warehouses stocked with goods from around the globe, was compared to wealthy Port Royal in Jamaica before the latter was wiped out by an earthquake.

The bulk of Barbados's 281,000 population lives in and around the capital, with an estimated 100,000 actually within the city and suburbs. The capital is the seat of the Barbados government, with the British monarch holding executive powers and represented on the island by a governor general, who in turn advises the cabinet and appoints the prime minister. Next come 21 members of the Senate and a 28-member House of Assembly, residing in the Parliament Buildings.

Most of the attractions can be seen in half a day on a walking tour starting near National Heroes Square (also known as Trafalgar Square (➤ 51), with the rest of the day spent shopping and trying out the cafés and restaurants. Bridgetown is also a base for day cruises, yacht charters, a trip on the Atlantis Submarine (➤ 144) and scenic helicopter flights (➤ 96). ✚ 2J

BRIDGETOWN SYNAGOGUE

Tucked away off Magazine Lane and
worth a visit is the Jewish Synagogue.
Next door is a Jewish cemetery where
weathered tombs contain the remains
of Jews who arrived in Bridgetown in
the 17th century and set up businesses
on nearby Swan Street. The synagogue
dates back to 1654, but was rebuilt in
the 19th century following extensive
hurricane damage. Remarkably well
kept by the Barbados National Trust, it
is believed to be one of the oldest
synagogues in the western
hemisphere. Inside, gorgeous wood
paneling is brightened by the light from
a quartet of brass chandeliers.
Members of the island's present
Jewish population still use the
synagogue on a regular basis.

✚ *Bridgetown 4c* ✉ Synagogue Lane, off
Magazine Lane ☎ Barbados National Trust,
426 2421 🕐 Mon–Fri 9–12, 1–4 💲 Free,
donations welcome 🚌 Fairchild Street

THE CAREENAGE

Alongside the Careenage – a narrow inner harbor at the mouth of the Constitution River – a wooden boardwalk accented with ornate, green-painted street lamps takes you past dozens of charter yachts and ocean-going boats advertising tours and deep-sea fishing. On the other side of the harbor are the many restored and painted houses of The Wharf. Toward the town, the boardwalk leads back to the main square or across Chamberlain Bridge to Independence Arch. Built in 1987, this monument commemorates the 21st anniversary of the island's independence.

✚ *Bridgetown 3e* ✉ The Wharf, off National Heroes Square ✋ Free 🍴 Waterfront cafés ($–$$) 🚌 Fairchild Street, main bus terminal

MONTEFIORE FOUNTAIN

The Montefiore Fountain, built in memory of a Jewish businessman called John Montefiore, was originally installed in Beckwith Place. Its position today, on what looks like a traffic island in Coleridge Street, seems inappropriate for such a beauty. Look closely and you'll see the figures of Fortitude, Temperance, Patience and Justice portrayed. The accompanying inscription reads, "Look to the end; Be sober-minded; To bear is to conquer; Do wrong to no one."

🕇 *Bridgetown 4b* ✉ Coleridge Street
🖐 Free 🚌 Fairchild Street

NATIONAL HEROES SQUARE

Best places to see ➤ 50–51.

PARLIAMENT BUILDINGS

Though Barbados has the third oldest parliament in the whole of the Commonwealth, established in 1639 with an all-white House of Assembly, the Parliament Buildings to the north of National Heroes Square are younger. This is due to the number of fires that blighted the town, the most devastating occurring in 1766. Following the fire of 1860, the Parliament Buildings you see now were built in neo-Gothic style. This group includes the Senate and the House of Assembly, the latter fitted with stained-glass windows depicting British monarchs and Oliver Cromwell. The clock tower is not the original; that was demolished in 1884 and a new one built two years later in 1886. Here sat the decision-makers, colonists of the 1700s busily reaping the rewards of sugar cane farming. You can imagine them fretting over whether the "mother country," England, would interfere with their right to self-government, or whether their slaves were plotting to rebel. The West Wing has been refurbished and there is talk of opening a National Heroes Gallery, but details were not available at the time of writing.

✚ *Bridgetown 5d* ✉ Top of Broad Street

a walk around Bridgetown

Begin at National Heroes Square (➤ 50) and exit the square along St Michael's Row for a look in St Michael's Cathedral (➤ 87).

Continue up St Michael's Row until you reach the gates of Queen's Park (➤ 86).

Stroll through the grounds, peer into the Georgian house, and find the African baobab tree.

Head back to National Heroes Square by the same route and turn right up Marthill Street. The road veers left and then right onto Magazine Lane.

You'll soon come to Synagogue Lane on the left, which leads to the Bridgetown Synagogue (➤ 80) and, behind a low wall to the right of the building, the Jewish cemetery.

Return to Magazine Lane, turning left toward the Montefiore Fountain (➤ 82).

Behind the fountain are the law courts, library and police station. Until they were closed in 1878, the law courts housed the Town Hall Gaol. Behind is Tudor Street, one of the oldest streets in the city.

Continue southwestward along Coleridge Street, turning right onto Swan Street. At the junction (intersection) with Milk Market turn left and continue until you reach the throng of Broad Street.

Once known as New England Street, Broad Street is Bridgetown's main thoroughfare, lined with stores selling

duty-free jewelry, rums, perfumes, leather goods and other tourist goods. An eyecatcher is the sugary pink-and-white Victorian facade of Da Costa's Mall.

At this point you can either take a detour right and stroll along the boardwalk around The Careenage (▶ 80), or continue to the starting point of the walk near the Nelson statue.

Distance Approximately 1.25 miles (2km)
Time 3 hours or half a day with lunch, shopping and rest stops
Start/End Point National Heroes Square ✚ *Bridgetown 5d*
✉ Fairchild Street
Lunch Waterfront Café ($–$$) (▶ 95)

QUEEN'S PARK

One of the attractions in the park is the 89ft-high (27m) baobab, estimated to be 1,000 years old and believed to have originated in Guinea, West Africa. Its circumference is 82ft (25m). In the pleasant park surrounding the baobab you'll see Barbadians in suits resting for lunch and children playing on the steps of the bandstand. The white Georgian building, Queen's Park House, was once the home of the commander of the British troops. It is now devoted to exhibitions of local arts and the theater.

✝ *Bridgetown 8c* ✉ End of St Michael's Row ⏱ Daily 🖐 Free
🚌 Fairchild Street

ST MICHAEL'S CATHEDRAL

The cool and tranquil cathedral, also known as the Cathedral Church of St Michael and All Angels, began as a small wooden church with enough scats for a congregation of 100 people. It was built between 1660 and 1665, but was destroyed by a hurricane in 1780 and had to be rebuilt. The new St Michael's became a cathedral when William Hart Coleridge, the first bishop of the island, arrived on Barbados in 1825.

www.stmichaelbarbados.com

✠ *Bridgetown 6d* ✉ St Michael's Row ☎ 427 0790 🕐 Daily 9–5 ✋ Free, donations welcome 🚌 Fairchild Street

More to see around Bridgetown

BARBADOS MUSEUM AND HISTORICAL SOCIETY

The Barbados Museum and Historical Society provides a wonderfully old-fashioned introduction to Barbados housing around 250,000 objects, including West Indian fine and decorative arts, pre-Columbian archaeological pieces and African objects.

Displays begin with the evolution of the planet and a showcase of coral, a major ecosystem of the island. Tools fashioned from coral by the Arawaks and Caribs are here, as are explanations of the tribes' religious beliefs. Fast-forward to the 1600s and you come to the arrival of the English colonists. From 1627 to 1640, until sugar cane flourished, tobacco and cotton were the main crops. Planters relied heavily on African slaves to develop the sugar economy and it is estimated that around 400,000 slaves were imported to Barbados between 1627 and 1807. Their skin was stamped with the initials of their white owner, using an instrument similar to the museum's silver slave-brand dated c1800. The museum explains how, after emancipation, slaves tried to make the transition to independent islanders through schooling, farming, entertainment and music.

Outside are examples of the island's architecture and a military gallery. Prints showing the days of slavery, bequeathed to the museum by shipping magnate Sir Edward Cunard, hang in a gallery also graced with shell displays. The African Gallery is now open and redesigned to link the Caribbean with its African ancestry. Of fascinating importance is a collection of rare West Indian books, plus early maps of Barbados including the earliest known map of the island, dated 1657.

www.barbmuse.org.bb

➕ 2K ✉ St Ann's Garrison, St Michael ☎ 427 0201 🕐 Mon–Sat 9–5, Sun 2–6 ♿ Inexpensive 🍴 Several cafés nearby 🚌 Fairchild Street, or from the south alight at Garrison Savannah ❓ Specially designed tours can be arranged. A Fine Craft Festival is held on the first Sat in Dec

GARRISON HISTORIC AREA

Best places to see ➤ 46–47.

GEORGE WASHINGTON HOUSE

After seven years of fund-raising and restoration, the house on
Bush Hill where a young George Washington spent seven weeks
in 1751 was opened to the public in January 2007. America's first
president traveled with his older half-brother, Lawrence, in search
of a more temperate climate to help the latter's tuberculosis. The
Washingtons also had connections with some of the prominent
families on the island.

The two-story Georgian-style house, perched on an escarpment
overlooking Carlisle Bay, now serves as a museum and interpretive
center and also features a genealogical center which can help
Americans trace their roots on the island. Over the centuries, the
building has also served as a private home, a base for French
prisoners, offices and part of the British military garrison.
www.georgewashingtonbarbados.org

➕ 2K ✉ Bush Hill, The Garrison, St Michael ☎ 228 5461 🕒 Mon–Sat
9–4:30 ♿ Inexpensive 🍴 Café and gift shop on site

MOUNT GAY RUM VISITOR CENTER

For the rundown on rum and a sip of the neat stuff, visit the
Mount Gay Rum Visitor Center and learn the story of what is
reputedly the home of the world's oldest rum (part of Remy-
Cointreau since 1989). This is actually the blending and bottling
factory; the distillery itself is in St Lucy, in the north of the island.
Step in to a traditional-style chattel house and learn about the
history of rum since 1703, right up to how it's aged, blended and
bottled today. If you book a special luncheon tour with one of the
sightseeing operators, or through your resort/hotel rep, then
transport, a Bajan buffet and a free miniature bottle of rum are
included. Of course, you can taste the rum in comfort at
the on-site shop. Note how the bottles line wooden shelves

behind the bar as they do in rum shops all over the island.

⊞ 1J ✉ Brandons, Spring Garden Highway, St Michael ☎ 425 8757
🕐 Daily 8–4:30, tours 9:30 and 3:30 ✋ Moderate 🚌 From Bridgetown, take
the Holetown bus to Brandons

PELICAN CRAFT CENTER

Between the cruise terminal and Bridgetown, this
small craft center is an interesting stop if you've
decided to walk between the two. Sitting on land
reclaimed from the sea, the center's pyramidal
roofs shelter shops selling local arts and crafts. It
also has workshops where you can watch some
of the island's finest craftspeople at work.
Metalwork, glassware, wooden crafts, pottery,
paintings and batiks come with a reasonable price tag. You can
also buy Royal Barbados Cigars made by the Caribbean Cigar
Company. There is also a restaurant, and a café serves breakfast,
lunch and afternoon drinks.

⊞ 1J ✉ Princess Alice Highway, Bridgetown ☎ 427 5350 🕐 Mon–Fri
10–5, Sat 9–2. Hours extend during peak holiday season ✋ Free 🍴 Cork and
Bottle Café ($)

ST PATRICK'S CATHEDRAL

The cornerstone of Roman Catholic St Patrick's Cathedral was originally laid in 1840, but because of lack of funds and too few Catholics, it wasn't consecrated until decades later, in 1899. The interior is dressed with Scottish marble, Irish crests and flags. Nearby, overlooking the Esplanade and Carlisle Bay, is a statue of social reformer and former prime minister Sir Grantley Adams. He stands outside the present government's headquarters and offices of the prime minister.

➕ 2J ✉ Highway 7, St Michael ⏰ Daily ✋ Free, donations welcome 🍴 Several choices ($–$$) on the coastal road 🚌 Take buses to Bridgetown or the south coast

TYROL COT HERITAGE VILLAGE

Just over 2.5 acres (1ha) of landscaped gardens encompass Tyrol Cot Heritage Village, said to be the birthplace of Barbadian democracy. Built in 1854, the house was home to the late Sir Grantley Adams, founder of the Barbados Labor Party, from 1929. He was the first premier of Barbados and the only prime minister of the short-lived West Indies Federation. Adams was one of the 10 national heroes named by the present prime minister, who also declared Adams's birthdate (April 28, 1898) National Heroes Day and a public holiday. Adams's son, Tom, who became prime

minister from 1976 to 1985, was born here. Restored by the Barbados National Trust, the house is built of coral stone blocks. Inside it still has the Adams's own Barbadian antique furniture. Within the

4-acre (1.5-ha) grounds is a craft village in the style of a traditional chattel house settlement – the moveable homes of plantation workers. You can buy handmade souvenirs by local artists here. There is a replica of an 1820s thatched slave hut revealing the simple way slaves lived in the days of the great sugar plantations.

🔳 2J ✉ Codrington Hill, St Michael ☎ 424 2074 🕐 Mon–Fri 9–5; shops may close earlier 👜 Inexpensive 🍴 The Rum Shop, on site 🚌 From Bridgetown, take the Cave Hill, Holders Green or Jackson bus

NB: See also Southern Barbados listings (➤ 146–153) for additional establishments in St Michael and Christ Church.

HOTELS

❦❦❦❦Hilton Barbados ($$$)

Recently refurbished, this 350-room Hilton resort is 1.5km (1 mile) from the center of Bridgetown, on the beach. It has an impressive lagoon pool, children's club, tennis courts and three restaurants, including the prestigious Careenage.

✉ Needham's Point, St Michael ☎ 426 0200; www.hiltoncaribbean.com

❦❦❦The Savannah ($$$)

Two hundred years old, directly on the beach at Hastings, 10 minutes from downtown Bridgetown and walking distance from Garrison Savannah, and part of the "Gems of Barbados" group. Luxurious rooms, with mahogany four poster beds in some. Go for the beachfront suites.

✉ Hastings, Christ Church ☎ 435 9473; www.gemsbarbados.com

RESTAURANTS

Aqua Restaurant and Lounge ($$$)

Hip, minimalist design, with Swedish and Bajan influences from the two owners, directly on the beach at Hastings. Eclectic menu with some Asian influences in the Thai curries, also incorporating everything from surf 'n' turf to sushi. Reserve in advance.

✉ Hastings Main Road, Christ Church ☎ 420 2995; www.aquabarbados.com

The Boucan Wine Bar and Restaurant ($$)

Situated at the pretty Savannah hotel with al fresco dining. Live music most nights and a traditional Barbadian Sunday brunch.

✉ The Savannah, Hastings, Christ Church ☎ 435 9473

Brandons Beach ($)

Just half a mile from Bridgetown port, serving lunch and dinner, including a big Sunday buffet. Serves grilled specialties, seafood and Bajan dishes. Right on the beach, with volleyball in the sand.

✉ Spring Garden Highway, St Michael ☎ 425 6450

The Careenage ($$$)

Elegant à la carte restaurant at the Hilton Barbados, serving grilled meat and seafood, Asian fusion and Caribbean dishes.

✉ Needham's Point, St Michael ☎ 426 0200; www.hiltoncaribbean.com

Champers ($$–$$$)

Set on the water's edge of Hastings, this popular wine bar and restaurant has a bistro downstairs and a pleasant dining room upstairs boasting fine views of the ocean.

✉ Skeetes Hill, Hastings, Christ Church ☎ 434 3463; www.champersbarbados.com 🕑 Daily lunch and dinner

Nelson Arms ($)

Here you'll find a mix of traditional English food – steaks and pies (steak and kidney for example) as well as Bajan fish dishes, also rice and burgers.

✉ Broad Street, Bridgetown ☎ 431 0602 🕑 Daily 8–6

Waterfront Café ($–$$)

Seafood specialties are served on tables spilling out onto the harborside. There's piano music on Tuesday in the afternoons and steel pan music or jazz from 7pm. See also Entertainment.

✉ The Careenage, Needham's Point, St Michael ☎ 427 0093; www.waterfrontcafe.com.bb 🕑 Mon–Sat 10am–midnight

SHOPPING

Colombian Emeralds International

Duty-free jewels from around the Caribbean, and emeralds from Colombia.

✉ Broad Street, Bridgetown; Grantley Adams Airport; Cruise Terminal; Almond Beach Village ☎ 1 800 6NO DUTY 🕑 Varies

Diamonds International Barbados

Similar to Colombian Emeralds. Have a diamond mounted and set before you leave.

✉ Broad Street, Cave Shepherd in Bridgetown; Fairmont Glitter Bay Hotel in St James; Grantley Adams Airport ☎ 430 2400 🕑 Mon–Sat

Kirby Gallery

A good place to pick up original art and limited-edition prints by local and international artists.

✉ The Courtyard, Hastings, Christ Church ☎ 430 3032, www.kirbyartgallery.com 🕐 Mon–Fri 9–1, 2–5

Markets

Barbados isn't noted for its markets, but the Saturday morning Cheapside Fruit Market (Lower Broad Street, Bridgetown) offers fruit, handicrafts, jewelry and Rastafarian curios.

ENTERTAINMENT

Waterfront Café

Lunchtime piano on Tuesdays, and either CD background jazz, live jazz, or steel pan music and singing on selected evenings.

✉ The Careenage, Bridgetown ☎ 427 0093 🕐 Mon–Sat 10am–midnight

Harbour Master Cruises

Evening dinner cruise featuring floor show of belly dancing, limbo and calypso.

✉ From Shallow Draught, Bridgetown ☎ 430 0900; www.tallshipcruises.com 🕐 Various nights; reservations essential

Jolly Roger Party Cruise

Fun sail on the wooden schooner; rope swing and snorkel.

✉ From Shallow Draught, Bridgetown ☎ 430 0900; www.tallshipcruises.com 🕐 Various, phone to book Thu and Sat

SPORT AND ACTIVITIES

Kensington Oval

Try and catch a live cricket match, the regional season runs January to March, while the international season is April to May.

✉ Kensington Oval, Bridgetown ☎ 436 1397

Bridgetown Heliport

Air-conditioned helicopters whisk you along the Caribbean coast.

✉ Bridgetown ☎ 431 0069; www.bajanhelicopters.com

Northern Barbados

In contrast to the south, the far north of the island is sleepy and undeveloped, covered with rippling sugar cane fields sloping down to small settlements on sandy beaches, or in the far north, craggy cliffs.

This is where the warm Caribbean meets the stormy, rough Atlantic Ocean and the scenery is reminiscent of how Barbados may have looked 100 years ago before tourism developed: goats and sheep in the fields, unassuming, often ramshackle little houses, many churches, the occasional rum shack and to the east, the wilder Scotland district which almost resembles the moorlands and rolling hills after which it is named.

Speightstown

Holetown

ANDROMEDA BOTANIC GARDEN
Best places to see ➤ 36–37.

ANIMAL FLOWER CAVE
The cave is at North Point, unsurprisingly as far north as you can go on Barbados. When you go you can expect a breezy and exposed, yet fabulous, spot for photography. A flight of steps leads down to a cavern carved out of the coral rock where there are scattered pools containing hundreds of sea anemones. Natural historian Griffith Hughes described them as animal flowers in 1750. Look behind you and the view of the ocean is amazing. Look down and you'll see the pools are deep enough to swim in, but be careful of the slippery surface.

➕ 2C 🗺 St Lucy ☎ 439 8797 🕐 Daily 9:30–5 ✋ Inexpensive 🍴 Café ($) serving snacks 🚌 From Bridgetown take the Connell town bus

BATHSHEBA
Best places to see ➤ 40–41.

BARBADOS POLO CLUB
Polo on the island dates back to the 1900s and was introduced by the British cavalry who, having tired of playing against each other, roped in the locals. The Barbados Polo Club was established at what is now the historic Garrison in Bridgetown in 1929 and moved in the 1960s to its current location on Holders Hill in St James with its wide grassland and towering trees. Recently, three new polo fields have been developed. Each year, from between October and the end of May, the season's itinerary includes fixtures against international teams, bolstered by Bajan hospitality. These matches are well attended by tourists, many of whom regard Barbados polo as one of the most vibrant sports on the island. Afternoon tea and cucumber sandwiches are served in style in the atmospheric wooden clubhouse after the game.

🕇 1H ⊠ Holders Hill, St James ☎ 427 0022 🖐 Free, but priced tickets for international matches

BARBADOS WILDLIFE RESERVE
Best places to see ➤ 38–39.

a drive along East Coast Road

The East Coast Road (also called the Ermie Bourne Highway) runs through the parishes of St Andrew and St Joseph between the Atlantic Ocean and the Scotland District. Opened in 1966 by Queen Elizabeth II, the road slithers along the route of the old railway from Bridgetown to Belleplaine and passes three of our Best Places to See.

Have your hotel prepare a picnic lunch beforehand so you can stop and spend an hour sitting on the sands and watching the surfers. Remember, it is too dangerous for swimming, but at low tide you can explore the rock pools.

Start from Bathsheba (➤ 40). Spend a while at Andromeda Botanic Gardens (➤ 36) and Bathsheba village before heading north, keeping the ocean to your right.

Worn, wooden chattel houses face deserted beaches scattered with rock formations and giant boulders. Next comes Cattlewash (➤ 40). The road here is not busy, so you can stop at intervals to take photographs. The Scotland District on your left, so called because it reminded British settlers of the Scottish Highlands, is a rugged area of steep lanes with sheep and cattle grazing on the hillsides. Many potters exploit the clay deposits in this area (➤ 42).

Drive on a little farther to reach a peaceful resting spot, Barclays Park, a picnic area popular with locals on public holidays. On weekdays, you might be the only visitor. The park was a gift from Barclays Bank in 1966, the year of independence.

This short drive ends at the village of Bellaplaine, where the railroad once terminated.

Distance 4 miles (6.5km)
Time Half a day with lunch and stops
Start Point Bathsheba ✚ 4F
End Point Bellaplaine ✚ 3E
Lunch Take a picnic or have a buffet at New Edgewater Hotel ($$) (➤ 121) ❓ The drive can be done in reverse and linked with part of the drive to the island's northern tip (➤ 110).

CHALKY MOUNT VILLAGE
Best places to see ➤ 42–43.

EARTHWORKS POTTERY
Earthworks Pottery is another showcase for Barbadian art crafted from local clay. Founded in 1983 as a small art studio making individual pieces, the pottery has expanded and now produces a range of trinket bowls, carvings and custom-made tiles – and yes – all major credit cards are accepted. It's a bright and cheerful place where practically everything except the trees and grass are

painted. There's also a batik studio and an art gallery. After touring the pottery and watching the artists, you can dine on light meals on the veranda next to a bamboo patch.

www.earthworks-pottery.com

✚ 2G ✉ St Thomas ☎ 425 0223 🕐 Mon–Fri 9–5 (except public hols), Sat 9–1 ✋ Free 🍴 Treehouse Café ($–$$, ☎ 425 0223) 🚌 From Bridgetown, take Hillaby or Shop Hill bus

FARLEY HILL NATIONAL PARK

Once the most imposing mansion on Barbados, 19th-century Farley Hill at Farley Hill National Park was built to show off the accumulated wealth of the sugar planters. Originally known as Grenade Hall, it came into the hands of Sir Thomas Graham Briggs, who named it Farley Hill. Amid the fire-damaged ruins, overgrown with plants, you can imagine the sumptuous parties held here during the heyday of the sugar boom. Prince Alfred, the second son of Queen Victoria, and Prince George (later George V of England) arrived in carriages to take luncheon or dinner. Though you can't enter the roofless house for safety reasons, you can get a good look at the ruins through its windowless frames. It makes a dramatic setting for outdoor jazz at the annual Barbados Jazz Festival in January. The park trail leads to a picnic spot overlooking the Scotland District and Atlantic coastline where you might hear the rustle of green monkeys in the treetops above.

➕ 2E ✉ St Peter ☎ 422 3555 🕐 Daily 8:30–6 👆 Inexpensive 🍴 Café ($) at Barbados Wildlife Reserve opposite 🚌 From Bridgetown, Speightstown and Bathsheba

FAIRMONT ROYAL PAVILION ESTATE

The west coast has many pseudonyms, "Platinum Coast," "Gold Coast" and even "Millionaires' Row," maybe because its sands are silvery or gold, and the hotels ultra-glamorous and extremely expensive. Commanding an historic estate is the Fairmont Royal Pavilion, where writers meet their publishers and where Sir Edward Cunard, one of the world's greatest shipping magnates, lived. Renowned South American-born landscape architect Fernando Tabora created the tropical gardens here. There is a weekly guided botanic tour of the courtyards, beds and lily ponds on Wednesdays at 10am. You follow the head gardener through more than 400 coconut trees. If you're stylishly dressed, you can take afternoon tea in the Café Taboras of the Royal Pavilion. In traditional 1930s manner, a white pot of Earl Grey, Darjeeling, peppermint or camomile tea is brought to your table, accompanied by a tiered stand of chocolate brownies, pastries, jam turnovers and crustless cucumber sandwiches.

✚ 1F ✉ Porters, St James ☎ 422 5555 ⏰ Tour at 10am Wed
🍴 Afternoon tea daily 3:30–5 🚌 From Bridgetown or Speightstown

FOLKESTONE MARINE RESERVE

Not solely of interest to scuba divers, the park tells the story of the marine life of the island through its museum. Here you'll learn interesting snippets: for example, did you know the sex of a sea turtle is

determined by the temperature of the sand the eggs are laid in? Then rent some equipment and go snorkeling in the sea to see fish, sponges and coral. Nearby, glass-bottomed boat tours will take you out to Dottins Reef wrecks and the reefs.

✚ 1G ✉ Folkestone, St James ☎ 422 2314 ⏱ Park open daily, museum Mon–Fri 9–5 💰 Park free, museum inexpensive 🍴 Beach bars, cafés and a picnic area 🚌 From Speightstown, Holetown and Bridgetown

FRANK HUTSON SUGAR MUSEUM

Yet another property run by the Barbados National Trust is the Sir Frank Hutson Sugar Museum. Its collection of old sugar objects and machinery and tells the story of what was once the most prized commodity on the island. The collection was started by Barbadian engineer Sir Frank Hutson and is a tribute to his passion. During the cane-grinding season, from February to May, you can step over to the boiling house at the Portvale Sugar Factory, one of a few factories still working on the island, for a dollop of molasses.

✚ 2G ✉ St James ☎ 426 2421 ⏰ Mon–Sat 9–5 (except public hols) ✋ Museum inexpensive, factory tour extra 🍴 Excellent cafés ($–$$) on the coast road 🚌 From Bridgetown take the Rock Hall bus

GRENADE HALL FOREST AND SIGNAL STATION

This is a good place to escape the relentless Caribbean sun. A trail descends through a web of vines and winds on for nearly a mile on paved paths smothered in moss. It's slippery, so wear strong soles with treads. At intervals you'll see questions (forming part of a quiz), plus quotes and anecdotes from the likes of Charles Darwin and an Amerindian chief. These remind us that humans continues to exploit the rainforests of the world for timber. There is a cave that sheltered Arawak Indians and, later, Rastafarians and escaped convicts. Shell tools found here are on display at the Barbados Wildlife Reserve (➤ 38).

Next door to the forest is the restored, whitewashed tower of the Grenade Hall Signal Station, built in 1819. Barbados had a string of such stations, established following the slave rebellion of 1816. During the uprising, one-fifth of the island's sugar cane fields was set on fire and scores of slaves were killed, executed or deported. The news of the revolt took hours to reach the authorities in Bridgetown, so the following year the governor proposed that a chain of signal stations be built to aid communication. The network relayed messages by flags, to which watchful messengers responded by dispatching the news to headquarters in

Bridgetown. Following the abolition of slavery, the signal stations'
crews passed the time by monitoring approaching cargo ships and
announcing school times. An audio tape plays as you browse
through displays of clay pipe fragments and musket balls. Climb
the polished wooden staircase to the lookout at the top and
imagine life before the telephone.

✚ 2E ✉ Farley Hill, St Peter ☎ 422 8826 🕓 Daily 10–5, last entry
3:30–3:45 (arrive before 3 to see the monkeys) ✋ Moderate; includes Forest
and Signal Station 🚌 From Speightstown

a drive to the island's northern tip

This drive covers the northern tip of the island, from the
parish of St Peter up to St Lucy.

*Head north on the coastal road out of Speightstown,
keeping the sea to your left. Pass the entrance to
Almond Beach Village and Port St Charles Marina and
turn right up a hill. Continue over the junction
(intersection) and look out for All Saints Church.*

Flanked by sugar cane fields, All Saints Church, built in
1649, is the resting place of William Arnold, the first
English settler. His grave is clearly marked.

*Continue to a T-junction (intersection), turn right and
follow signs to the Barbados Wildlife Reserve (▶ 38).*

Farley Hill National Park (➤ 103) appears first, to your left. Park inside and walk around the ruins. Leave the car where it is and cross the road to the Barbados Wildlife Reserve. After seeing the animals, birds and reptiles, have a drink or snack in the café before exploring nearby Grenade Hall Forest and Signal Station (➤ 108).

Leave Farley Hill and follow signs to the Morgan Lewis Sugar Mill (➤ 114) and Cherry Tree Hill. Stop by St Nicholas Abbey, the island's oldest house. You can then loop back to the main road into St Lucy and onto the Animal Flower Cave (➤ 98) and North Point.

At stunning North Point take tea and photos until it's time to head back on the coastal road to Speightstown.

Distance Approx 16 miles (26km)
Time Half a day with lunch, to a full day
Start/End Point Speightstown ✚ 1E
Lunch Barbados Wildlife Reserve ($) ❓ If you plan to walk the forest nature trail, wear sturdy shoes and be careful on the mossy paths

HARRISON'S CAVE

Best places to see ➤ 48–49.

HOLETOWN

You can spend a full day in Holetown or, during
February, a full week at the annual Holetown
Festival. The festival coincides with the landing of
the first British settlers to the island on February
17, 1627. Prior to this, English Captain John Powell,
sailing the *Olive Blossom* to Brazil, anchored off the
small natural harbor and set foot at what he
declared Jamestown. Later, the settlement was
renamed "the Hole" after a tiny inlet where boats
could harbor. Back in England, Powell reported his
discovery to his employer, Sir William Courteen, an
Anglo-Dutch merchant. Courteen responded by
sending out an expedition of about 80 settlers and
a group of African slaves captured from a Spanish
galleon. Powell headed the mission, sailing the

William and John. More white settlers followed, setting up home and establishing crops of cotton, ginger and tobacco. They soon found out how to tend and utilize the soil using methods taught to them by Arawak Indians brought over especially from Guyana. Commemorating the landing is the Holetown Monument on the forecourt of the town's police station, the former fort. The date, for some reason, mistakenly reads 1605.

Around the town are a few buildings dating from the 17th century. St James was the first church, originally built of wood. Inside is the old font and a bell inscribed "God Bless King William, 1696." Modern gems include the exceptional Patisserie Flindt (► 59), plus a chattel village of craft shops and an art gallery.

➕ 1G ✉ St James 🍴 Excellent cafés and bars ($–$$) 🚌 From Bridgetown, Speightstown and Bathsheba

MORGAN LEWIS SUGAR MILL

At one time Barbados had many
wind-driven mills. They were
introduced by the Dutch planters
from Brazil when they brought
sugar cane to the island in the
1600s, flattening the forests to
make way for vast plantations
worked by slaves from Africa. The mills crushed the sugar cane to
extract the juice, which would then go through a process of boiling
and cooling before finally ending up as sugar for export. Built
around 1776, the restored Morgan Lewis Sugar
Mill is the largest complete windmill in the
Caribbean. It is set within a working farm and
occupies a gorgeous location, flanked by a row of
mahogany trees. Inside is the grinding machinery,
made by a firm in Derby, England. Although not as
vital as tourism, the sugar industry is still
important to Barbados.

✚ 2D ✉ Near Cherry Tree Hill, St Andrew ☎ 422 7429
🕒 Mon–Sat 9–5 ✋ Moderate

ST NICHOLAS ABBEY

Just beyond the magnificent lookout of Cherry Tree Hill in
St Andrew, St Nicholas Abbey is a wonderful, Jacobean-style
plantation house, believed to be one of only three still standing in
the western hemisphere and recently beautifully renovated. The
house was built in 1650 and is supposedly the oldest in Barbados,
although it was never an abbey. During the days of slavery, it was
a working sugar plantation. Its past is riddled with scandal; the
original owner, Colonel Benjamin Berringer, was killed in a duel
with his neighbor, John Yeamans, after Yeamans had an affair with
Berringer's wife. Yeamans then married the wife but the two fled
the island in 1669 for Carolina, unable to cope with the prejudices

of the day, and Yeamans became governor of the colony after only three years.

Guided tours of the ground floor take place, to see the cedar paneling, Dutch gables and Chinese Chippendale staircase.

www.stnicholasabbey.com

🔳 2D 🖂 Cherry Tree Hill, St Peter
☎ 422 8725 🕙 Daily 10–3:30
🖐 Inexpensive

SIX MEN'S BAY

At the coastal village of Six Men's Bay wooden fishing boats, waiting to be treated or repaired, are pulled up onto the grass beyond the shoreline. Nets and floats lie scattered about, as do chunks of mahogany used by boatbuilders to make the keels. If you're lucky, you might see work being carried out. Usually the boatbuilders don't mind if you stop to chat or ask questions. Pretty wooden houses line one side of the road while the sea laps the sands opposite, making this a refreshing place to rest before reaching Speightstown.

🔳 1E 🖂 Near Speightstown 🍴 Rum shops and restaurants in Speightstown ($–$$) 🚌 Speightstown bus from Bridgetown

SPEIGHTSTOWN
Best places to see ➤ 52–53.

WELCHMAN HALL GULLY
Formed by a series of caves that collapsed, the gully is a 0.62-mile (1km) corridor of tropical jungle cutting through the coral foundations of the island. Cliffs rise up on either side, and banana, nutmeg and fig trees are among the 200 or so species of tropical plant that grow in the gully. It is said to take its name from a Welsh settler called Williams who once owned the land through which the ravine cuts. His descendants planted some of the trees.

The National Trust, which takes care of the site, has added a few plants but it's pretty much left in a wild state. As you walk through, it is easy to imagine how Barbados must have looked before the first settlers arrived and carried out a program of ravaging deforestation. At one end a stalactite and stalagmite have met in the middle to form a 46-in (118-cm) diameter column that appears to be holding up the cliff. If you're present around dawn or dusk, you might spot Barbados green monkeys.

✚ 2G ✉ St Thomas ☎ 438 6671 ⏰ Daily 9–5 (except public hols)
👋 Moderate 🚌 From Bridgetown take the Sturges bus ❓ Wear good walking shoes and take drinking water

a walk along the Arbib Nature and Heritage Trail

The Arbib Nature and Heritage Trail – run by the Barbados National Trust – won the Caribbean ecotourism award, beating entrants from 20 other islands. There are two trails of varying length: the longer "Whim Adventure" trail cuts through the Whim Gully, one of many ravines of limestone and coral that lead to the sea and drain the island's rainfall. Get the most from the trail by taking a guided walk.

The trail begins from Speightstown (although it isn't well marked) and passes villages, sugar cane plantations and cottonfields. As you go, the guide stops to point out herbs and other plants that have medicinal uses, such

as the castor-oil plant. You will weave through mango, banana and grapefruit trees, dog's dumpling, breadfruit, the bearded fig and a pumpkin patch.

In the interior villages you'll see Barbadian chattel houses (the traditional homes of plantation workers), some with their own kitchen gardens. The chattel is built perfectly symmetrically with a door in the center and windows either side. Traditionally the roof is made of shingle, with a steep pitch to allow rain to run off easily. Surprisingly, these tiny buildings withstand hurricanes pretty well, too.

As the walk nears the coast the houses become grander. You can rest near the cannon at the remains of 18th-century Dover Fort, overlooking the waterfront apartments of Port St Charles, before heading back to Speightstown. Stroll back along the sandy beach in front of the Almond Beach Village before joining your guide for a drink at the rum shop at Speightstown harborside.

Distance 5 miles (8km); alternative 3.5 miles (5.5km) trail
Time 2 or 3.5 hours, depending on stops
Start/End Point Speightstown ➕ 1E
Lunch Various places in Speightstown ($–$$)
❓ Walks operate Wed, Thu, Sat at 9:30 and 2:30 and must be reserved. Wear proper walking shoes, a sun hat, sunscreen and take drinking water (☎ 426 2421)

HOTELS

☷☷Almond Beach Club and Spa ($$)

Luxurious, adults-only all-inclusive on the west coast in a romantic setting, with a lavish spa; a grown-up alternative to the family Almond Beach Village farther north.

✉ Vauxhall, St James ☎ 432 7840; www.almondresorts.com

☷☷☷Almond Beach Village ($$–$$$)

An all-inclusive resort consisting of 395 rooms and suites within a historic sugar plantation, originally built in 1865, close to the sea. Ideal for families, with a spa, fitness classes, tennis and golf lessons, and masses of children's facilities (➤ 74).

✉ St Peter ☎ 422 4900; www.almondresorts.com

☷☷☷Cobblers Cove ($$$)

Pink turrets rising from manicured, tropical green foliage distinguish this Relais et Chateaux property perched above coral sands. Cottages and suites, furnished with cottons and rattan furniture, open onto gardens or the sea. The ultimate, though, is a seafront suite with rooftop plunge pool (➤ 74).

✉ St Peter ☎ 422 2291; www.cobblerscove.com

Colony Club ($$$)

A former gentleman's club, the Colony is now a sophisticated hotel with an old Englishness and charm catering to both couples and families. The extensive tropical gardens include four freshwater pools.

✉ Porters, St James ☎ 422 2335; www.colonyclubhotel.com

☷☷☷Coral Reef Club ($$)

A family-run and owned hotel which offers great service and fine dining in a colonial plantation setting (➤ 74).

✉ St James ☎ 422 23 72 (booking agent); www.coralreefbarbados.com

☷☷Crystal Cove Hotel ($$)

Small hotel with bright, whimsical design in colours of the Caribbean, overlooking a pretty pool and beach. Romantic dining –

and a swim-up bar inside a cave, behind a waterfall (➤ 74).

✉ Porters, St James ☎ 432 2683; www.crystalcovehotelbarbados.com

♦♦♦♦Fairmont Royal Pavilion Hotel ($$$)

Although a beachfront resort, this rose-pink, graceful top-price establishment is very private. It is shrouded in tropical gardens so diverse that it takes a botanical tour (held weekly) to explain the species. Enjoy the afternoon tea of cakes and cucumber sandwiches, served in a traditional, 1930s English style (➤ 75).

✉ Porters, St James ☎ 422 5555/422 0118; www.fairmont.com

♦♦♦The House at Tamarind Cove ($$$)

A very exclusive, adults-only sanctuary for luxury and privacy. The hotel has just 34 rooms, and ambassadors, who are similar to butlers, on hand to provide the best service (➤ 75).

✉ Paynes Bay, St James ☎ 432 5525; www.thehousebarbados.com

New Edgewater Hotel ($$)

Set on a ledge overlooking the Atlantic crashing onto rock formations below, the New Edgewater, one of the few hotels on the east coast, is only a few steps from Bathsheba beach. Voted Best Small Hotel by readers of *Caribbean Life* magazine. Ideal for experienced surfers or anybody looking for a quiet, relaxed, glitz-free vacation.

✉ Bathsheba beach ☎ 433 9900; www.newedgewater.com

♦♦♦The Sandpiper ($$)

Just 20 minutes from Bridgetown in Holetown, this charming beachfront hotel, set amid landscaped grounds, offers individual suites for families and couples. Facilities include a top-class restaurant, pool, tennis and water sports. Member of the Small Luxury Hotels of the World (➤ 75).

✉ Holetown, St James ☎ 422 2251; www.sandpiperbarbados.com

♦♦♦♦Sandy Lane ($$$)

Unashamed luxury, this famous hotel has accommodated royalty and movie stars in its luxurious rooms and suites since 1961. The

Palladian-style cream coral stone buildings are situated in a beautiful 800-acre (324-ha) beachfront estate (➤ 75).

✉ St James ☎ 444 2000; www.sandylane.com

Treasure Beach ($$)

Boutique, all-inclusive hotel set in lush tropical gardens right by a white sand beach (➤ 75).

✉ Paynes Bay, St James ☎ 432 1346; www.treasurebeachhotel.com

RESTAURANTS

L'Acajou ($$$)

Sandy Lane's main restaurant redesigned by internationally acclaimed David Collins is now well established. Formal dining on the terrace with sea views. European fare with hints of Asia.

✉ Sandy Lane, St James ☎ 444 2030; www.sandylane.com ⏰ Daily 6:30–10pm

♦♦♦Calabaza ($$$)

Moroccan-style architecture, overlooking the ocean creating a very romantic atmosphere. Mix of Eastern and Western cooking.

✉ Prospect St James ☎ 424 4557; www.calabazabarbados.com ⏰ Dinner daily

Carambola ($–$$)

An outstanding setting on a cliff above the sea. Caribbean dishes influenced by France and Asia make this a favorite with Bajans.

✉ Derrick's, St James ☎ 432 0832 ⏰ Mon–Sat 6:30–9:30pm

♦♦♦♦The Cliff ($$$)

Regarded as the finest, most expensive and most exclusive restaurant on the island, The Cliff has a neoclassical, tiered dining terrace overlooking the sea. Each dish is a masterpiece. Booked up for months in advance.

✉ Derrick's, St James ☎ 432 1922; www.thecliffbarbados.com ⏰ Mon–Sat 6:30–9:30pm

⛀⛀⛀Daphne's ($$$)

Grilled specials and seafoods with an Italian influence are featured at this elegant contemporary restaurant, sister to Daphne's in London. Famous cocktails and an extensive wine list.

✉ Payne's Bay ☎ 432 2731; www.daphnesbarbados.com ⏲ Daily 12:30–3, 6:30–10:30

The Fish Pot ($$)

A regular haunt in the north for A-list celebrities who dine at this water's edge restaurant in part of a converted fort on the beach. As the name suggests, fish-oriented menu.

✉ Little Good Harbour, Sherman's ☎ 439 3000 ⏲ Daily lunch and dinner

⛀⛀⛀Lone Star Restaurant and Hotel ($$–$$$)

Stylish beach restaurant offering eclectic Mediterranean, modern European and traditional Caribbean dishes from meze to curries, served al fresco (► 75).

✉ Mount Standfast, St James ☎ 419 0599; www.thelonestar.com
⏲ Daily 11:30–3:30, 6–10

Mango's By the Sea ($$)

Romantic setting overlooking the ocean and known for its lobster bisque and grilled lobster. Also serves New York strip steak and barbecued back ribs followed by home-made desserts and excellent espresso.

✉ By the sea, Speightstown, St Peter ☎ 422 0704;
www.mangosbythesea.com ⏲ Daily 6–9:45

Mannie's Suga Suga Beach Bar ($$–$$$)

A great setting above the coral sands of Mullins Beach, one of the most famous beaches on Barbados. Breakfast, light lunches and romantic candlelit Thai and Japanese dinners are available.

✉ Mullins Bay, St Peter ☎ 419 4511; www.mullinsbeach.com
⏲ Daily 9am–10pm

⛀⛀Olives Bar and Bistro ($$)

Cozy garden patio bistro with tables laid out under fairy lights.

Seafood, jerked pork and scorched onions, steaks and pizza.

✉ 2nd Street, Holetown, St James ☎ 432 2112 🕐 Nightly 6:30–9:30

Palm Terrace ($$$)

Romantic, Moorish-style restaurant within the Fairmont Royal
Pavilion serving international food on fine china at candlelit tables.
The sound of the lapping waves add to the atmosphere.

✉ Fairmont Royal Pavilion Hotel, St James ☎ 422 5555; www.fairmont.com
🕐 Mon–Sat 7am–9:45pm. Afternoon tea ($) for non-guests served 3:30–5

Patisserie Flindt ($)

A great place to sit with a coffee or glass of wine. The cakes are
divine and created by Savoy-trained Carsten Flindt (➤ 59) .

✉ Holetown, St James ☎ 432 2626; www.flindtbarbados.com 🕐 Mon–Fri
7am–5pm, Sat 7am–2pm, Sun (in season) 7am–midnight

Round House Inn & Bar ($)

Sandwiches, soups, quiches and seafood, Monday to Saturday.
Take in the great views with your lunch.

✉ Bathsheba ☎ 433 9678; www.roundhousebarbados.com.

Sassafras ($–$$)

Gorgeous setting in a restored plantation house near Holetown.
Caribbean ingredients with an Asian twist are used to great effect
in the good value set-price menu.

✉ Derricks, St James ☎ 432 6386; www.sassafras246.com 🕐 Lunch
Mon–Fri, daily dinner

Il Tempio ($$)

Traditional Italian cuisine on the beach in a romantic setting.
Patronized and admired by Pavarotti.

✉ Fitts Village, St James ☎ 417 0057; www.iltempiorestaurant.com
🕐 Tue–Sun 12–2:30, 6:30–10; closed Aug and Sep

The Terrace Restaurant ($$$)

A well-recommended Relais et Chateaux restaurant within
Cobbler's Cove Hotel. Continental food with a Caribbean accent is

prepared by French-trained chefs and served on a romantic terrace by the sea. Friday night is a fish and caviar extravaganza. Great cocktails and a renowned wine list are highlights. Reservations essential.

✉ Cobbler's Cove, St Peter ☎ 422 2291; www.cobblerscove.com ⏱ Daily 12:30–2:30, 6:30–9

❖❖❖The Tides ($$$)

Set on the water's edge overlooking the sea with an excellent menu of chowders, salads, pasta, seafood and the fresh catch of the day; there's also an imaginative vegetarian menu. Try the bistro-style restaurant inside for casual dining or the terrace outside for a more romantic setting in lush gardens.

✉ Holetown, St James ☎ 432 8356, www.tidesbarbados.com ⏱ Lunch Mon–Fri, dinner Mon–Sat

SHOPPING

Cave Shepherd Sunset Crest Mall

A good selection of souvenirs, clothing, gifts, crafts and curios.

✉ Sunset Crest Plaza No. 2, Holetown ⏱ Mon–Sat

Chalky Mount Village

Best places to see ➤ 42–43.

Colombian Emeralds International

Broad range of beautiful emerald, diamond and gemstone jewelry; designer Italian gold and exquisite watches.

✉ Sandy Lane, St James ☎ 419 4505 ⏱ Times vary

Earthworks Pottery

See pottery, from bowls to ornaments, being made and hand-decorated. Also clay, metalwork, glass and fabric designs (➤ 102).

✉ Edgehill, St Thomas ☎ 425 0223; www.earthworks-pottery.com ⏱ Mon–Fri 9–5, Sat 9–1

Gourmet Shop at Chattel Village

Edible treats from Bajan hot sauce, nutmeg and vanilla beans to

aged bourbons. Hand-rolled Cuban cigars also available.
✉ Chattel Village, Holetown ☎ 432 7711 🕒 Mon–Sat 9–5:30

Mango's Fine Art Gallery
Works by local artist Michael Adams, who grew up in Africa and
graduated from the Royal College of Art, London.
✉ Queen Street, Speightstown ☎ 422 0704 🕒 Daily 6–11:30pm

Shell Gallery
An outstanding collection of shells from around the world.
✉ Contentment, Gibbs, St Peter ☎ 422 0943 🕒 Mon–Fri 9–5, Sat 9–2

ENTERTAINMENT
Casbah
Moroccan-style nightclub with DJ music and regular live music.
Dress code. Valet parking.
✉ Baku Beach, Holetown ☎ 432 2258 🕒 Thu–Sat 10pm–4am

Coach House
Busy pub with live entertainment and sports from around the
world via satellite.
✉ Paynes Bay, St James ☎ 432 1163 🕒 24 hours; Happy Hour 5–7pm

Fisherman's Pub and Beach Bar
The Sunset steel orchestra and floor show is on regularly, plus
Bajan buffet every Wednesday evening.
✉ Speightstown, St Peter ☎ 422 2703 🕒 Open for drinks nightly

SPORTS AND ACTIVITIES
Island Safari
Exciting adventure tours with knowledgable local guides.
✉ Bush Hall Main Road, St Michael ☎ 429 5337; www.islandsafari.bb

Sandy Lane Country Club Course
Open to all golfers on a pay-as-you-play basis. Stunning views of
the west coast. Correct attire essential.
✉ St James ☎ 444 2500

Southern Barbados

In the south of Barbados you will find the bustling capital, Bridgetown, and the airport, with attractions coming thick and fast between the two, all within easy reach of one another. Inland, however, forested terrain slopes upward to Gun Hill, from which there are amazing views right across the island.

Oistins

On the coast, dramatic cliffs rise up past South Point Lighthouse, sandy beaches and big rollers at their base, attracting surfers. The island's party scene is along the southwest coast at St Lawrence Gap, a fun-packed strip of bars, clubs, craft stalls, rum shacks and less expensive hotels, ideal for a family vacation.

BANKS (BARBADOS) BREWERIES

Wherever you go on the island you'll see black, red and white billboards announcing that, apart from rum, the only thing to drink on Barbados is Banks beer. During a tour of the brewery and "Brew-seum", just outside Bridgetown, you can see it being brewed, visit the old brew house and have a tasting. Notice that the copper kettles, used for the brewing process for 30 years, have been replaced by modern steel vats that can each hold 3,080gal (14,000L) of beer. Even more astounding is the bottling hall, where 250,000 bottles of Banks are capped each day.

➕ 2J ✉ St Michael ☎ 228 6846 🕐 Tours: Mon–Fri 10, 12 and 2. Closed Wed ✋ Inexpensive 🍴 Bar for beer tasting, cafés and restaurants ($–$$$) in Bridgetown 🚌 From Bridgetown

BARBADOS CONCORDE EXPERIENCE

A brand new attraction situated at Grantley Adams International Airport, giving visitors a chance to find out all they ever wanted to know about Concorde, which used to fly regularly to the island.

There's an interactive flight school, a departure lounge, an observation deck, and a multimedia interactive presentation projected along the entire length of the aircraft and including live sound effects of Concorde taking off and breaking the sound barrier. Visitors can see the cockpit and a simulator, view historic photos of the aircraft and buy memorabilia in the gift shop.

➕ 4K ✉ Grantley Adams International Airport, Christ Church 🕐 Daily 9–6 ✋ Moderate

THE CRANE

Try to visit this historic hotel on a Sunday morning so you can enjoy the brunch and foot-tapping live gospel by local singers. It takes place in the clifftop terrace restaurant overlooking the cliffs and the Atlantic. On one side is the hotel pool: the majestic white colonnades surrounding a circle of blue and backed by the ocean have been photographed by dozens of fashion magazines. On the other side, sheer cliffs drop to the pink sands of Crane Beach.

Opened in 1887 on the site of an 18th-century mansion and lit by oil lamps, The Crane was the first resort hotel on Barbados. At that time, ladies bathed discreetly in a specially built area called "the horse." The original steps cut into the cliff, leading to "the horse," still remain. As for the name of the hotel, it came about when there was a small commercial port here and a crane was used to raise and lower cargo on and off the trading ships that docked.

✚ 5J ✉ Crane, St Philip ☎ 423 6220 ⏰ Brunch Sun 9:30am; singing Sun 10–11am; Bajan buffet Sun 12:30–3. Advance reservations essential 🍴 Restaurant ($$–$$$) noted for its seafood, especially oysters 🚌 From Bridgetown catch the Sam Lord bus

GRAEME HALL BIRD SANCTUARY

Just down the road from the lively St Lawrence Gap is an unlikely
setting for a bird sanctuary, but this beautiful mangrove swamp is
an oasis of calm in comparison to the coastal strip. The Graeme
Hall Swamp is the island's largest expanse of inland water, home
to two types of mangrove and 40 species of bird from sandpipers
to cattle egrets. Follow the boardwalks around the swamp and
look for green monkeys, mongoose and in the water below, tarpon

fish. There is an enclosed area where you can admire the scarlet ibis, parrots and flamingos. Information boards tell you about the trees and there's a migratory bird exhibit. It's a great afternoon out for families, painters, photographers, birdwatchers or anybody looking for a tranquil place simply to sit and contemplate the scenery.

www.graemehall.com

✚ 2K ✉ Worthing ☎ 435 9727 🕐 Daily 8–6 🍴 Café and shop ($)

GUN HILL SIGNAL STATION

Even if you've already visited Grenade Hall Signal Station (➤ 108) and learned about the signal stations' important role in the early communications network of Barbados, Gun Hill Signal Station is still worth a visit for the views. It was built in 1818 and was reputedly the cream of the string of stations established to warn of slave uprisings. Eventually they served as lookouts for cargo ships. Restored by the Barbados National Trust in 1982, Gun Hill, perched on a ridge overlooking the St George Valley and the south of the island, features a gray flag tower. For travelers with time it's a quiet place to while away a few hours or wait for the best views, which occur around sunset. Look for the British Military Lion, a white figure carved from limestone in the 19th century by the adjutant-general of the Imperial Forces, who was stationed on the island. A plaque below the lion states his name and reads that the British lion shall "...rule from the sea to the ends of the earth."

✚ 3H ✉ St George ☎ 429 1358 🕐 Mon–Sat 9–5 🍴 Café ($); opening hours restricted 🚌 From Bridgetown take the Sergeant Street bus

HERITAGE PARK AND FOURSQUARE RUM DISTILLERY

Voted by a newspaper in the United States as "one of the most modern rum distilleries in the world," the Heritage Park and Foursquare Rum Distillery comes complete with its own integrated recycling plant. If that alone isn't a sufficient draw, there is plenty more to see at this attraction, which covers 7 acres (3ha) of a once sprawling sugar plantation and includes one of the island's oldest sugar factories. In an outdoor museum filled with machinery, you can see how rum was made in the early days, or you can go underground to the furnace and feel what it was like to be a boiler worker. Nowadays, the distillery is known for its top-selling ESAF White Rum, Orland Brigand and Doorly's Rum, which, naturally, you are given the opportunity to taste.

Capitalizing on the popularity of the Heritage Park, there are exhibitions of paintings by local artists in the on-site art galleries. There are also demonstrations of glass blowing and screen printing, and regular lunch and dinner cultural shows in the Cane Pit Amphitheatre.

➕ 5J ✉ Foursquare, St Philip ☎ 420 1977 🕐 Mon–Fri 9–5 👊 Moderate; includes access to the beach 🍴 Sugar Cane Café ($–$$) 🚌 From Bridgetown take the St Patrick bus ❓ 40-minute tour available for cruise parties only who book in advance

OCEAN PARK AQUARIUM

Ocean Park is a relatively new project, with 26 displays of marine life from the Caribbean and beyond. Great care has been taken to create natural settings, including fresh water pools and piranha tanks set into rocks, a stand of mangrove trees and a living reef, under which a perspex tunnel has been set. There's a big tank containing nurse and blacktip reef sharks, which are fed every day, and an open-air touch pool where children can handle living starfish and conches. In addition, there's an adventure playground, mini golf, a gift shop and a small café serving fantastic fruit smoothies. www.oceanparkbarbados.com

✚ 4K ✉ Balls, Christ Church ☎ 420 7405 🕐 Summer Tue–Sun 10–6; winter daily 10–5 👋 Moderate 🍽 Café ($–$$)

OISTINS

By day, Oistins is a busy fishing village that supplies fresh fish and shellfish to the whole of the island. Boats are forever landing catches or are pulled up on the grassy sand dunes for repair or paintwork. Walk among the lobster pots and nets, then watch the fishmongers gutting and packing the fish in ice at the fish terminal. You can get a cheap bite to eat here at lunchtime, but the real draw is the enormously popular Friday night Fish Fry, when stallholders fry flying fish, dolphin, shark, barracuda and snapper. Order your fish with rice or a helping of macaroni cheese pie and a bottle of Banks beer. There's music, long lines at the counters and dancing by the tables. Saturday nights are also popular, but even better is the Oistins Fish Festival, which runs over Easter.

✚ 3K ✉ Christ Church 🍽 Excellent freshly fried fish at stalls ($)
🚌 From Bridgetown

ORCHID WORLD

Best places to see ➤ 44–45.

RAGGED POINT

An old lighthouse marks Ragged Point, the most easterly point of the island. It is a wonderfully exposed, tranquil spot. Though the lighthouse is no longer open to the public, its beams still warn ships away from the limestone cliffs and Cobbler's Reef. Slightly to the north of the lighthouse is tiny, uninhabited Culpepper Island, Barbados's only "colony".

✚ 6H ✉ St Philip 🍴 Cafés and restaurants ($–$$$) en route 🚌 To Crane Beach or Sam Lord's Castle 🖐 Free

ST GEORGE VALLEY

St George Valley is an agricultural oasis covered with sugar cane fields. St George Parish Church stands proudly as one of only four churches on the island to survive the hurricane of 1831. Built in 1784, the church boasts a splendid altar painting called *Rise to Power*. It is the work of artist Benjamin West, the first American president of the Royal Academy. And remember the statue of Lord Nelson in Bridgetown? Well, the sculptor, Richard Westmacott, also created some sculptures here inside the church.

✚ 3H

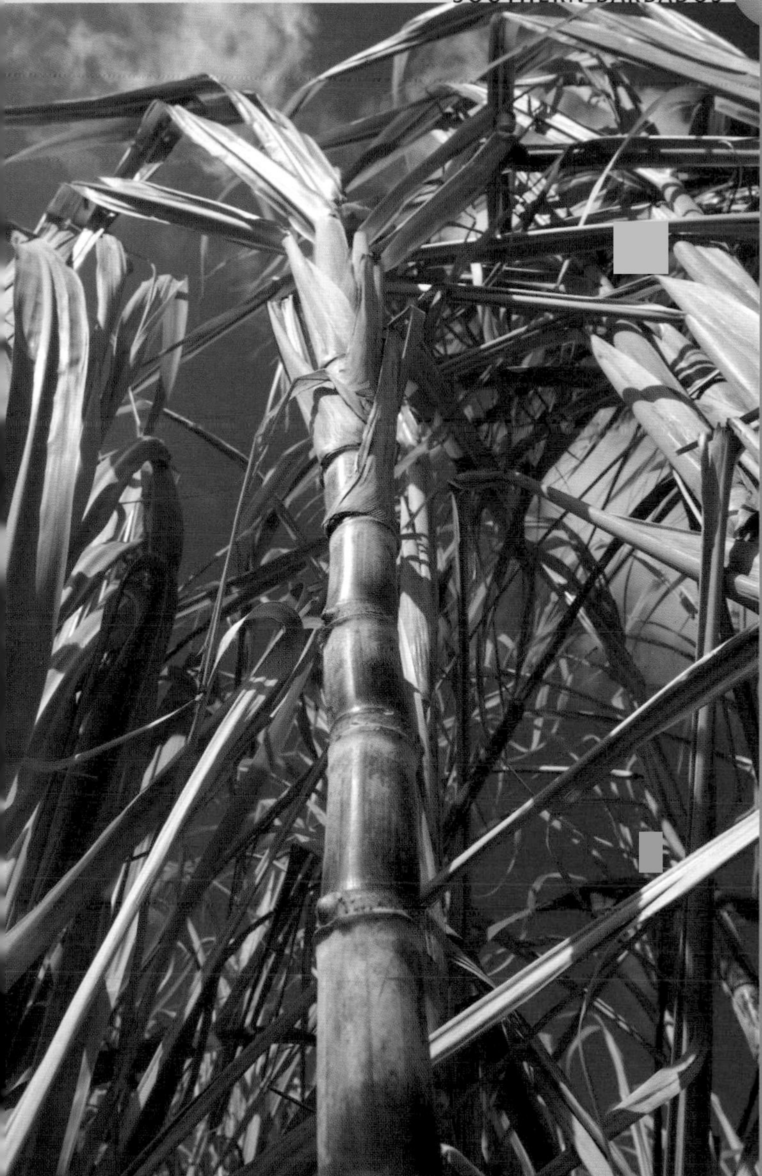

a drive and Sunday brunch

One Sunday morning, having reserved tickets in advance, skip breakfast and head along the south coast to hear gospel singing at The Crane hotel (➤ 129). En route you'll see Bajan women in dresses, hats and white gloves attending church. Some men wear their Sunday best suits. Quietly and unobtrusively, stop outside any church and listen to the hymns.

Start from Oistins (➤ 135) on the Maxwell main road and head east, following the signs to the airport. You'll drive through villages with painted houses and cane fields. Follow the signs to Crane Beach.

Arrive at The Crane hotel at 9:30am in time for Sunday brunch at 10:30 and enjoy the entertainment (advance reservations are essential). Afterward, walk down to Crane Bay for swimming, sunbathing or body boarding.

Drive out of Crane Beach and head north finishing up at Ragged Point (➤ 136) for a brief walk and lunch (if you're still hungry).

On the drive back you can take a right detour to Sunbury Plantation House (➤ 54) for afternoon tea before heading back towards Oistins.

If the day is still young, take a left detour through small communities to reach Silver Sands beach (➤ 141).

Watch the windsurfers flip 360 degrees above the waves. Look for the South Point Lighthouse, made in England out of cast iron and shipped in pieces to the island. It was reassembled and working by 1852.

Alternatively, head straight back along the coastal road to Oistins fishing village for the perfect finale – a succulent fish fry in the open air at one of the many shacks.

Distance Approx 7 miles (12km) **Time** Half a day with brunch and stops
Start Point Oistins ✚ 3K **End Point** Ragged Point ✚ 6H
Brunch The Crane hotel ($$) (➤ 129)

ST LAWRENCE GAP

Moving westward along the south coast, the closer you get to Bridgetown the livelier it becomes. St Lawrence Gap is where the party people go, although regulars say it's not as friendly and easy-going as it used to be. Sports bars with video screens, live blues, happy hours and karaoke, souvenir shells and painted maracas are what it's all about. There's a string of good restaurants and, in between the hotels and apartment buildings, crescents of sandy beach and safe swimming. You can learn to dive, water-ski or just hang on to a banana boat.

➕ 2K ✉ South coast, east of Bridgetown 🍴 Bars and restaurants ($–$$), some with live music 🚌 Any south coast bus from Bridgetown

SILVER SANDS

Silver Sands beach at the southern tip of the island is a Mecca for professional windsurfers, and there's a Club Mistral center here for lessons and equipment rental. In addition to windsurfing you can try boogie boarding, hiking and wilderness and adventure diving. As the beach's name suggests less adventurous types can relax on the beautiful silver sands and watch others hard at play.

✚ 4L ✉ Silver Sands, Christ Church
🍴 Snacks ($) nearby

SUNBURY PLANTATION HOUSE

Best places to see ➤ 54–55.

WILDEY HOUSE

Wildey House, a Georgian hilltop mansion set in beautiful grounds, is the headquarters of the Barbados National Trust. Although the building is not in the best state of repair, visitors will see historic photographs of Barbados and exquisite silver displayed among antique furniture in carefully decorated rooms. The Trust is important to the island because it enables its architecture,

sometimes dating back more than 350 years, to be preserved and maintained. Since 1961 the Trust has taken on the care of eight properties, including a wooded gully (➤ 116), the largest sugar mill in the Caribbean (➤ 114) and a botanic garden (➤ 36). It has also helped to create an underwater park (➤ 106) on the west coast and has identified Bush Hill (➤ 47, 90) as the house in which George Washington, president of the United States, stayed in 1751.

✚ 2J ✉ Wildey, St Michael ☎ 426 2421 ⏱ By appointment

A submarine cruise

an excursion

There are few places in the world where you can board a real submarine and submerge for an undersea exploration. Complete with Captain Nemo-style sounds and live dialogue between the crew and the surface, the Atlantis Submarine trip is pricey, but shouldn't be missed.

First, you board the *Ocean Crest* catamaran and sail out of Bridgetown's harbor to reach the submarine. Safety instructions are given before you are invited to board.

In 1994 *Atlantis* became the world's first passenger submarine. Stretching 66ft (20m) and displacing 80 tons, the *Atlantis III* sinks slowly to 151ft (46m). It then cruises gently above the seabed off the west coast at 1.5 knots. You sit with the other passengers on benches, facing outward through large portholes.

The seabed is white, like fallen snow. A wreck appears, the fish darting in and out of its gaps. Next comes a garden of brain coral, ferns and sponges. If you're lucky, a turtle might glide gracefully by. You'll definitely see thousands of fish, from stingrays to barracudas and shoals of colorful species. If you've ever wanted to scuba dive but lacked the courage, this is the next best thing.

Even more spectacular is Atlantis By Night, a cruise taken when the coral is at its most striking and nocturnal predators come out to feed. The submarine's lights

illuminate the coral and fish and you'll see the wreck of the *Lord Willoughby*. Whichever trip you take, at the end you're given a certificate to prove that you took the plunge.

Time 1 hour
Start/End point Atlantis Submarines ⊠ Shallow Draught, Bridgetown ☎ 436 8929; www.atlantisadventures.com
🖐 Expensive 🚌 Nearest bus station is Bridgetown; take a taxi to the harbor ❓ Book through Atlantis Submarines, a tour operator, or your hotel or resort rep. **Lunch** Sublime Café ($)

HOTELS

♦♦♦Accra Beach Hotel and Resort ($–$$)

An elegant hotel set on a spectacular beach of soft white sands, hosting cocktail parties, barbecues and floor shows. New wing of suites and pool suites now open.

✉ Christ Church ☎ 435 8920; www.accrabeach.com

♦♦♦Bougainvillea Beach Resort ($$–$$$)

Overlooking the Caribbean this luxury resort features suites with kitchen facilities. There are a choice of restaurants, kids' club, pool, water sports and tennis facilities.

✉ Christ Church ☎ 418 0990; www.bougainvillearesort.com

♦♦♦The Crane ($$$)

This 18th-century hotel perched on a cliff overlooks a pink bay, one of the island's most famous beaches (► 129).

✉ St Philip ☎ 423 6220; www.thecrane.com

♦♦Plumtree Club ($)

A resort condominium and apartments to rent nestled in lush, tropical gardens and close to restaurants and the Rockley Golf Course (► 153). Pool.

✉ Christ Church ☎ 435 7606; www.barbadosplumtreeclub.com

♦♦♦South Beach Resort and Vacation Club ($$)

New, ultra-modern boutique resort with just 49 suites. Not directly on the beach but has lounge chairs on Rockley Beach, at Splash Beach Bar.

✉ Rockley at Accra Beach, Christ Church ☎ 435 8561; www.southbeachbarbados.com

Turtle Beach ($$)

All-inclusive family resort with lively entertainment and a beautiful beach, perfect for young surfers.

✉ St Lawrence Gap ☎ 428 7131; www.turtlebeachresortbarbados.com

RESTAURANTS

Brown Sugar ($$–$$$)

Enjoy Bajan cuisine amongst lush ferns and a water garden. Highlights on the à la carte evening menu include the Creole fish chowder, pepper chicken and the coconut beer shrimp. A buffet lunch is available Sunday to Friday.

✉ Aquatic Gap, Bay Street, St Michael ☎ 426 7684; www.brownsugarbarbados.com

♦Bubba's Sports Bar and Restaurant ($)

Air-conditioned eatery with satellite screens showing major sporting events, serving local and international cuisine.

✉ Rodeley, Christ Church ☎ 435 6217; www.bubbassportsbar.net ◷ Daily lunch and dinner

♦Café Sol Mexican Grill and Margarita Bar ($)

A crowded yet fashionable haunt, specializing in big plates of nachos, salads and the typical Mexican fare, plus tall cocktails and occasional offers deals such as two-for-one drinks special.

✉ St Lawrence Gap, Christ Church ☎ 435 9531 ◷ Tue–Sun lunch, daily dinner

Croton Inn ($–$$)

Take your pick here from specials, curries, fish, and local specialty pudding and souse dish (pig, potatoes and pickle) on Saturday afternoons, and live jazz on occasions.

✉ Maxwell Main Road, Christ Church ☎ 428 7314; www.crotoninn.com ◷ Daily 6am–10:30pm

Flying Fish Restaurant and Bar ($–$$)

A bistro within the Yellow Bird Hotel overlooking St Lawrence Bay. Award-winning cuisine includes flying fish prepared eight ways, as well as traditional English fare and Lobster Night on Saturdays.

✉ St Lawrence Gap, Christ Church ☎ 418 8444; www.yellowbirdhotel.com ◷ Daily breakfast, lunch and dinner

♛♛♛Josef's ($$$)

Extravagant seafood dishes and wines from around the world in this very classy signature restaurant by the beach. Kampai Japanese Restaurant upstairs.

✉ St Lawrence Gap, Christ Church ☎ 420 7638; www.josefsinbarbados.com
🕐 Daily 6:30–9:30/10pm

Lucky Horseshoe ($–$$)

Open 24 hours for steaks, omelettes and waffles, a "trail blazing" BBQ buffet, spare ribs, pasta, rice and potatoes.

✉ Worthing Main Road, Christ Church ☎ 435 5825; www.luckyh.com
🕐 24 hours

Oistins Fish Market ($)

Amazing fish fry on Friday and Saturday evenings, when diners dance among the tables. At stalls and huts, freshly caught flying fish, dolphin, snapper, barbecued pig and chicken are cooked to take away or you can eat at the handy benches and tables (► 135).

✉ Oistins village, Christ Church 🕐 Mostly at night, some stalls are open throughout the day

♛♛Opa's Greek Restaurant ($$–$$$)

Family-run; authentic moussaka, calamari and souvlaki, with views of the ocean.

✉ Hastings, Christ Church ☎ 435 1234 🕐 Daily from 6pm

The Restaurant at Southsea ($$$)

Beautiful, romantic setting, exceptional food and multiple awards. Asian-influenced menu includes ostrich and alligator, although there's a tempting vegetarian selection, too. Book well in advance.

✉ St Lawrence Gap Road, St Lawrence Gap ☎ 420 7423; www.therestaurantatsouthsea.com 🕐 Daily for dinner

Ship Inn ($)

A good choice for a meal or a night out; for food choose between the Captain's Carvey or The Restaurant with an à la carte selection.

For late-night eating choose Barnacle Bill's BBQ which offers hearty sandwiches, burgers and hot dogs. See also Entertainment ➤ 152.

✉ St Lawrence Gap ☎ 420 7447; www.shipinnbarbados.com 🕓 Daily until late; Happy Hour 4–6pm, 10–11pm

Steak House Barbados ($–$$)

Here US sizzling steaks are served on signature cast-iron "cows," and there's also a salad bar, pasta, seafood, chicken and lamb. On the same site, St Lawrence Pizza Hut offers pizzas and hamburgers.

✉ St Lawrence Gap, Christ Church ☎ 428 7152; www.steakhousebarbados.com 🕓 Daily 9am–11pm

☗Sweet Potatoes ($–$$)

Friendly, clean and well-priced restaurant with Bajan specialties and cocktails. Happy hour 10–11pm.

✉ St Lawrence Gap, Christ Church ☎ 420 7668; www.thegapbarbados.com/sweetpotatoes 🕓 Daily

☗☗Wytukai ($$)

Exotic Polynesian atmosphere as you dine in an indigenous-style hut. Polynesian food and music.

✉ Accra Beach Hotel, Christ Church ☎ 435 8920; www.accrabeachhotel.com 🕓 Tue–Sat 6:30–11:30

☗☗Zafran ($$$)

Unique to Barbados, this authentic Indian restaurant is housed in an elegant mansion house set in extensive gardens with mango and coconut trees. Excellent Indian, Persian and Thai dishes are prepared by award-winning chefs and served in luxury surroundings, but not necessarily at luxury prices.

✉ El Sueno, Worthing Main Road, Worthing ☎ 435 8995 🕓 Daily

SHOPPING

Big B
Fresh meat, fruit, vegetables, a deli, a French bakery, a pharmacy and a bank, all in one place.
✉ Peronne Plaza, Worthing ☎ 435 7927 🕐 Mon–Thu 8–8, Fri–Sat 8–9

Chattel House Shopping Village
Colorful chattel-style houses crammed with souvenirs and beachwear bearing slogans such as "Jammin' in de Street."
✉ St Lawrence Gap, Christ Church (also at Holetown) ☎ 428 2472
🕐 Mon–Sat 9–6

Flamboya
Hand-painted, hand-dyed and appliquéd clothing, plus batiks.
✉ DaCosta's Mall, Broad Street, Bridgetown and Hastings Plaza, Christ Church ☎ 422 4098 🕐 Mon–Fri 8:30–5, Sat 8:30–3

Medford Craft Village
Woodcarvers create items from the mahogany trees and roots that surround them. Showroom with a host of Barbadian crafts.
✉ Barbarees Hill, St Michael ☎ 427 3179 🕐 Daily 9–5 (Sat until 2)

Sheraton Centre
Some 75 shops for clothing, gifts and electrical goods.
✉ Near Garfield Sobers Roundabout, near St Lawrence, Christ Church
🕐 Mon–Sat 9–9

ENTERTAINMENT

St Lawrence Gap, Christ Church, is the throbbing heart of Barbados, with clubs, bars and restaurants open until late. Happy hours are usually hosted early evening. It is best to arrive at a nightclub well after 10pm. Local live bands are highly talented.

39 Steps Wine Bar
Relaxing wine bar with live jazz every other Saturday night.
✉ Chattel Plaza, Hastings, Christ Church ☎ 427 0715 🕐 Mon–Fri noon–midnight, Sat 6pm–midnight

After Dark
Popular nightclub with indoor and outdoor dance floors with a range of music including DJ sets, Caribbean rhythms, a quieter jazz club and regular live bands.
✉ Christ Church ☎ 435 6457 ⏰ Fri– Sat night

Bert's Bar
Catch up with sports and world news live on satellite television. Popular slot machines and a famous daiquiri drink.
✉ Rockley, Christ Church ☎ 435 7924; www.bertsbarbados.com ⏰ Daily until 1am, happy hour Mon–Fri 4:30–6pm

Bajan Roots and Rhythms
A Caribbean show, carnival, extravaganza and dinner party, buffet and unlimited drinks.
✉ Plantation Theatre, St Lawrence ☎ 428 5048, www.theplantation.bb ⏰ Various, phone to book

Boatyard
Live bands, DJs and special events, with "free drinks" deals.
✉ St Michael ☎ 436 2622; www.theboatyard.com ⏰ 9am–late

Casuarina Beach Club
Regular live music by local bands, a steel orchestra and special West Indian floor shows.
✉ St Lawrence Gap ☎ 428 3600; www.casuarina.com ⏰ 24 hours

Club Skyy
New nightclub with the latest sounds and dance trends.
✉ Spring Garden, St Michael ☎ 421 7599 ⏰ Thu–Sat from 10pm

Coach House
Choose from the sports bar with live sports from around the world via satellite or stay on the beach for direct service straight from the beach bar. Al fresco dining is offered at the restaurant as well.
✉ Paynes Bay, St James ☎ 432 1163, www.thecoachhousebarbados.com ⏰ 24 hours; Happy Hour 5–7pm

The Crane

Amazing gospel singing and brunch (➤ 129) that's become an island institution. Advance reservations are essential.

✉ St Philip ☎ 423 6220, www.thecrane.com ⏰ Sun 9:30–noon

Harbour Lights

Massively popular beach-front club. Monday is Beach Party with BBQ, exotic drinks, live music, limbo and fire-eating. Wednesdays and Fridays are pay once, drinks free. Dance under the stars or indoors. The only nightspot where beachwear is acceptable, in fact, it's a must!

✉ Bay Street, St Michael ☎ 436 7225; www.harbourlightsbarbados.com ⏰ Mon, Wed, Fri, from 9:30pm–very late ❓ Minimum age 18

McBridges Pub and Cookhouse

Live music and dancing every night in popular Irish pub with an extended happy hour between 11pm and 1am. Food is also available in the form of pizzas, burgers, ribs and British/Irish-style pub food.

✉ St Lawrence Gap ☎ 435 6352; www.mcbridesbarbados.com ⏰ Daily, music 10pm–late

Reggae Lounge

Reggae, calypso and other Caribbean hits played by the island's DJs to a packed dance floor in the open air. Regular live bands.

✉ St Lawrence Gap ☎ 435 6462 ⏰ Nightly

Ship Inn

Traditional English-style pub with satellite sports and live music nightly, covering all bases from calypso to rock and soul. Karaoke is also a favorite. See also ➤ 59, 149.

✉ St Lawrence Gap ☎ 435 6961 ⏰ Daily until late; Happy Hour 4–6pm, 10–11pm

Whistling Frog

Solid street pub with occasional live music and DJ.

✉ St Lawrence Gap ☎ 420 5021 ⏰ 24 hours

SPORTS AND ACTIVITIES

Barbados Golf Club
In the south of Durrants close to the airport. Par 72, pay-as-you-play course redesigned in 2000 and since hosted the Barbardos open twice.

✉ Durrants, Christ Church ☎ 428 8463, www.barbadosgolfclub.com

Ocean Park Aquarium
This new aquarium attraction, geared toward families, takes an educational slant. See fish and marine life from the Caribbean, a living reef, ray pool and touch pool and feeding demonstrations. On site restaurant and bar. See also ➤ 135.

✉ Balls, Christ Church ☎ 420 7405; www.oceanparkbarbados.com
🕐 Summer Tue–Sun 10–6; winter daily 10–5

Rockley Golf and Country Club
Rockley is the oldest club on the island and has a pleasant 9-hole course offering pay and play.

✉ Rockley, Christ Church ☎ 435 7873, www.rockleygolfcourse.com

Surf Barbados
Surf tours, lessons and rentals for adults and children over 8 to suit a range of abilities. A maximum tutorial group of four people per instructor allows for more personal lessons.

✉ Varies according to surf conditions ☎ 256 3906; www.surfing-barbados.com

Index

Acknowledgements

The Automobile Association wishes to thank the following photographers for their assistance in the preparation of this book.

Abbreviations for the picture credits are as follows – (t) top; (b) bottom; (l) left; (r) right; (c) centre; (AA) AA World Travel Library

4l Mullins Bay, AA/J Tims; **4c** Heroes Square, Bridgetown, AA/J Tims; **4r** Rock formations, Bathsheba, AA/J Tims; **5l** Fairmont Royal Pavilion Hotel, AA/J Tims; **5c** Boardwalk, St Lawrence, AA/J Tims; **6/7** Mullins Bay, AA/J Tims; **8/9** Souvenirs, Bathsheba, AA/J Tims; **10/11t** Palm trees, Bottom Bay, AA/J Tims; **10cr** Souvenirs, Bathsheba, AA/J Tims; **10bl** Andromeda Botanic Gardens, AA/J Tims; **10br** Oistin's Friday night Fish Fry, AA/J Tims; **11cl** Shop, Speightstown, AA/J Tims; **11bl** Race Day, Garrison Savannah, AA/J Tims; **11br** Handbags, Holetown festival, AA/J Tims; **12/13t** Filleting flying fish, Six Men's Bay, AA/J Tims; **12bl** Hot Sauce on sale, AA/J Tims; **12br** Detail of breadfruit, AA/J Tims; **13tr** Bajan bread, AA/J Tims; **13cr** Green bananas, AA/J Tims; **14tl** Oistin's Friday night Fish Fry, AA/J Tims; **14bl** Mount Gay Rum, AA/J Tims; **14br** Advertising, Banks Brewery, AA/J Tims; **15tl** Cocktails, AA/J Tims; **15cl** Coconut ready to drink, Bottom Bay, AA/J Tims; **15cr** Round House Bar, Cattlewash, AA/J Tims; **16/17t** Souvenir stalls, Bridgetown, AA/J Tims; **16c** Turtle, Oistins, AA/J Tims; **16b** Coastline, Bathsheba, AA/J Tims; **17tr** Statue, Crane Beach, AA/J Tims; **17b** Oistin's Friday night Fish Fry, AA/J Tims; **18/19t** Sunset, Paynes Bay, AA/J Tims; **18/19b** Foursquare Rum Distillery & Heritage Park, AA/J Tims; **19br** Andromeda Botanic Gardens, AA/J Tims; **20/21** Heroes Square, Bridgetown, AA/J Tims; **24** The Holetown Dooflicky festival, AA/J Tims; **25** Cruise ship, AA/D Lyons; **26** Helicopter, AA/L K Stow; **27** Bus, Bathsheba, AA/J Tims; **28** Taxi, AA/J Tims; **29** Telephone box, AA/J Tims; **30** Policeman, AA/J Tims; **32** Sightseers looking over the Atlantic, AA/P Baker; **34/35** Rock formation, Bathsheba, AA/J Tims; **36cl** Andromeda Botanic Gardens, AA/J Tims; **36cb** Hibiscus Café, Andromeda Botanic Gardens, AA/J Tims; **36/37c** Andromeda Botanic Gardens, AA/J Tims; **37tr** Talipot Palm trees, Corypha umbraculifera, Andromeda Botanic Gardens, AA/J Tims; **38c** Barbados Green or Vervet monkey, AA/J Tims; **38bl** Two iguanas, Barbados Wildlife Reserve, AA/J Tims; **39t** Mahogany bar area, Barbados Wildlife Reserve, AA/J Tims; **39c** Goose, Barbados Wildlife Reserve, AA/J Tims; **40c** Surfing, Bathsheba, AA/J Tims; **40/41b** East Coast near Cattlewash, AA/J Tims; **41t** Shop, Bathsheba, AA/J Tims; **42** Highland Pottery, Chalky Mount Village, AA/J Tims; **43t** View from the Highland Pottery, Chalky Mount Village, AA/J Tims; **43cr** Vase, Highland Pottery, Chalky Mount Village, AA/J Tims; **43br** Bar, Chalky Mount Village, AA/J Tims; **44l** Red Ginger Flower, Alpinia purpurata, Flower Forest, AA/J Tims; **44/45c** Tropical corridor of palms, Flower Forest, AA/J Tims; **45r** Flower Forest, AA/J Tims; **46l** Garrison Historic Area, AA/J Tims; **46/47c** St Ann's Fort, Garrison Historic Area, AA/J Tims; **47t** Race Day, Garrison Savannah, AA/J Tims; **48/49** Harrison's Cave, Tony Arruza/CORBIS; **50b** Fountain, National Heroes Square, Bridgetown, AA/J Tims; **51tr** Nelson's Monument, National Heroes Square, Bridgetown, AA/J Tims; **51cr** War Memorial, Heroes Square, Bridgetown, AA/J Tims; **52b** Pier, Speightstown, AA/J Tims; **52/53t** Speightstown, AA/J Tims; **53c** St Peter's Parish Church, Speightstown, AA/J Tims; **54t** Prints of paintings by Augustino Brunias (1771), Sunbury Plantation House, AA/J Tims; **54cl** Study, Sunbury Plantation House, AA/J Tims; **54cl** Bath, Sunbury Plantation House, AA/J Tims; **55b** Sunbury Plantation House, AA/J Tims; **56/57** Outdoor dinning area, Fairmont Royal Pavilion Hotel, AA/J Tims; **58/59** Round House Bar, Cattlewash, AA/J Tims; **60/61** Accra or Rockley beach, AA/J Tims; **63** Mullins Bay, AA/J Tims; **64** Cobblers Cove, AA/J Tims; **65tr** Mullins Bay, AA/J Tims; **66/67b** Dive boat, Bridgetown, AA/J Tims; **67tr** Air tanks, AA/J Tims; **68/69** Bathsheba, AA/J Tims; **70** ABC

Highway, AA/J Tims; **71** Freed Slave statue, ABC Highway, AA/J Tims; **72** Jeep tours, Bathsheba, AA/J Tims; **73** Tourist with catch of Wahoo, Careenage, Bridgetown, AA/J Tims; **74** Harbour, Speightown, AA/J Tims; **76/77** Boardwalk, St Lawrence, AA/J Tims; **79** War memorial, Heroes Square, Bridgetown, AA/J Tims; **80tl** Bridgetown Synagogue, Bridgetown, AA/J Tims; **80/81** The Careenage, Bridgetown, AA/J Tims; **81br** The Careenage, Bridgetown, AA/J Tims; **82** Montefiore Fountain, Bridgetown, AA/J Tims; **83t** Detail, Parliament buildings, Bridgetown, AA/J Tims; **83b** Parliament buildings, Bridgetown, AA/J Tims; **84/85t** Interior of St Michael's Cathedral, Bridgetown, AA/J Tims; **85b** The Careenage, Bridgetown, AA/J Tims; **86/87t** Queen's Park, Bridgetown, AA/J Tims; **86bl** Bandstand, Queen's Park, Bridgetown, AA/J Tims; **87tr** Stained glass, St Michael's Cathedral, Bridgetown, AA/J Tims; **87b** St Michael's Cathedral, Bridgetown, AA/J Tims; **88** Garrison Historic Area, Barbados Museum, Bridgetown, AA/J Tims; **91t** Work of art for sale at the Indigenous Potteries, Pelican Craft Village, Indigenous Potteries/AA/J Tims; **91b** Pelican Craft Village, Bridgetown, AA/J Tims; **92b** Pottery, Chattel House Village, Tyrol Cot Heritage Village, AA/J Tims; **93** Chattel House Village, Tyrol Cot Heritage Village, AA/J Tims; **97** Farley Hill National Park, AA/J Tims; **98t** Animal Flower Cave, AA/J Tims; **98b** North Point, Animal Flower Cave, AA/J Tims; **99t** Barbados Polo Club, AA/J Tims; **101t** Near Cattlewash, AA/J Tims; **101b** Round House Bar, Cattlewash, AA/J Tims; **102bl** Path to Earthworks Pottery, AA/J Tims; **102br** Pottery for sale, Earthworks Pottery, AA/J Tims; **103t** Farley Hill Mansion, AA/J Tims; **104t** Fairmount Royal Pavilion Hotel, AA/J Tims; **105** Pool, Fairmount Royal Pavilion Hotel, AA/J Tims; **106/107t** Beach, Folkestone Marine Park and Museum, AA/J Tims; **106b** Folkestone Marine Park and Museum, AA/J Tims; **107b** Frank Hutson Sugar Museum, AA/J Tims; **108tl** Grenade Hall Forest, AA/J Tims; **109b** Grenade Hall Forest Signal Station, AA/J Tims; **110** View over Scotland District, Farley Hill National Park, AA/J Tims; **111** Animal Flower Cave, AA/J Tims; **112/113t** Holetown Chattel building, AA/J Tims; **112bl** Holetown Festival, AA/J Tims; **114tl** Barrels for Mount Gay Rum, AA/J Tims; **114/115c** House, Six Men's Bay, AA/J Tims; **115r** Six Men's Bay, AA/J Tims; **116/117** Welchman Hall Tropical Park, AA/J Tims; **118** Harbour promenade, Speightstown, AA/L K Stow; **119** Arbib Nature and Heritage Trail, AA/L K Stow; **127** Night view, St Lawrence, AA/J Tims; **128t** Banks Brewery, AA/J Tims; **128/129c** Crane Beach Hotel, AA/J Tims; **129b** View from Crane Beach Hotel, AA/J Tims; **130/131** Egret Island, Graeme Hall Nature Reserve, AA/J Tims; **132/133b** Views from Gun Hill Signal Station, AA/J Tims; **133t** Foursquare Rum Distillery & Heritage Park, AA/J Tims; **134** Fishing boats, Oistins, AA/J Tims; **135** Oistin's Friday night Fish Fry, AA/J Tims; **136** Ragged Point lighthouse, AA/J Tims; **137** Sugar cane, St George Valley, AA/J Tims; **138l** Filleting fish at Oistins fish market, AA/J Tims; **139t** House, Ragged Point, AA/J Tims; **139b** Crane beach, AA/J Tims; **140/141b** Rum shop, St Lawrence, AA/J Tims; **141t** Dover beach, St Lawrence, AA/J Tims; **142/143b** Wildey House, AA/J Tims; **143t** Reading room, Wildey House, AA/J Tims; **144/145** *Atlantis* submarine, AA/L K Stow

Sight locator index

This index relates to the maps on the covers. We have given map references to the main sights of interest in the book. Grid references in italics indicate sights featured on town plans. Some sights within towns may not be plotted on the maps.